Ariana Gee and Ma

C000040067

Be Your Own
Love
Coach

Ways to help you find and keep your soulmate

NH
NEW
HOLLAND

First published in 2005 by New Holland Publishers (UK) Ltd
London · Cape Town · Sydney · Auckland

www.newhollandpublishers.com

10 9 8 7 6 5 4 3 2 1

Garfield House, 86–88 Edgware Road, London W2 2EA, United Kingdom

80 McKenzie Street, Cape Town 8001, South Africa

14 Aquatic Drive, Frenchs Forest, NSW 2086, Australia

218 Lake Road, Northcote, Auckland, New Zealand

ISBN 1 84330 895 9

Publishing Manager: Jo Hemmings
Senior Editor: Kate Michell
Editor: Gillian Somerscales
Assistant Editor: Rose Hudson
Cover Design: Ian Hughes
Design: Gülen Shevki-Taylor
Production: Joan Woodroffe

Reproduction by Modern Age Repro Co, Hong Kong
Printed and bound Replika Press PVT Ltd, India

contents

Foreword

Putting the welcome mat out for love and relationships

Deep in our hearts we know that relationships offer the promise of heaven, but often they lead us to the experience of hell. We can easily feel like we want to give up on them. But actually every place we want to give up can be a new birthing place, a place of transformation, learning and growth to a point when we have the courage to face unpleasant feelings so we can move past them into greater happiness. Relationships can reveal to us our gifts and talents, the beauty of our heart and soul, the beauty of others and also the other sides of us that we find less attractive.

It's easy to get lost and even give up on relationships because most of us have never learned how they work, how to communicate effectively and how to grow within them. We get caught in past mistakes and can stay trapped for a lifetime. And yet the purpose of relationships is to be happy, fulfilled and to experience love, but that path is also strewn with pitfalls and obstacles.

We need to understand that relationships are the fast track to personal growth in our life. Nothing reveals our own light and dark sides more than a close relationship. We all find them challenging and we know in our heart the rewards and delights they also offer us. The secret is to know how to navigate the challenges and use them as tools for transformation. With awareness and skills, every place we stumble can be a place we can grow, but we need a map and a good guide to the territory.

In this book, Ariana and Mary have created that guide, and they are two great coaches to help you through and share the journey with you. They went on ahead, made the same mistakes that we've all made, and are now reporting back on how they learned. They have produced something unique, a guide that is both inspiring, hopeful and intensely practical; it will help you become aware of your inherited patterns of thinking and feelings so that you can make some new and life-affirming choices. Ariana and Mary help you to know that there is nothing wrong with you and that you are worthy and deserving of love if you will allow yourself to receive it. They help you know that within you is the capacity to love and to flourish in relationships, and that the only problem is your inherited conditioning.

One of the most powerful challenges they pose is 'How good will you let your relationship be?' Paradoxically, many of us don't have the welcome mat out for all the good things that we consciously say we want. Once things get a little too good we unconsciously begin to sabotage our good fortune, feeling either guilty or that we don't deserve it. We push away the very thing we have been chasing. Let Ariana and Mary coach you to release that guilt and pain in order to receive all the good things that are waiting for you, right now. The power is in your hands to transform your thinking and open the doors. So, let Ariana and Mary be your guides to the love and joy that is your birthright. Let yourself be blessed with loving relationships – it's what you were born for. Say 'Yes!' today.

God bless on your journey of relationships.

Nick Williams, London, August 2004

Nick Williams is the Director of Alternatives at St James's, London – a premier venue in Britain for major authors and workshop leaders from around the world. He is Founder of the Heart at Work project, author of the much acclaimed The Work We Were Born to Do *and an internationally established workshop presenter.*

Introduction

Become the chooser in your life

Do you want to find your soulmate without selling out on yourself? Or maybe you think you've found them, but just want to double-check that they're the one for you.

The chapters in this book provide you with a series of insights and exercises through which you can reflect on your experiences of love and relationships to date, separate the things that work for you and the things that are holding you back from achieving the quality of loving relationship that you really want and give you some practical tools to use so that you can put yourself into the position of chooser in your life, love and relationships.

Some of the principles and practices we promote may seem a little analytical to apply to so elusive and intangible a thing as love; but they have all been proved to make a massive difference in creating relationship and life success for those of our clients and friends who have committed to following them in their search for a soulmate.

If it's broke – fix it!

Societies and attitudes have changed radically over the past 30 years or so. Strategies that may have helped our parents' generation to find long-lasting love are not as effective in today's world, in which something like four in ten of all marriages end in divorce. Isn't it perhaps time to take a different approach to how we mate and relate, so that we improve the chances of creating enduring relationships that are truly loving and intimate?

Our purpose in coming together to write this book is to offer a different perspective on how to approach finding a partner, creating love in our lives and moving into a long-term committed relationship. We hope it will radically change the way you think about these things.

Both of us have a background in psychology, are qualified practitioners in Neuro-Linguistic Programming, graduate coaches with CoachUniversity and specialize in relationship development. Ariana was a couples counsellor with Relate and Mary is a personal development and organizational consultant, having studied for an MSc. in the psychology of human change. Between us we have over 30 years' experience of working in this area. We are also both divorcees, and it is in our own lives that we have gained the greatest experience of learning and growth. We have hands-on experience of the pain and distress that failed relationships bring, not only to ourselves and our partners, but also to our children and stepchildren.

By sharing our own experiences and those of our clients, friends and colleagues, we want to offer you an approach to creating love in your life and relationships which will help you to:

- develop a genuine love and regard for yourself;
- create a great life for yourself, whether in a relationship or not;
- establish what it is you are seeking in a soulmate;
- develop strategies for going out and finding that special person;
- learn how you can check out if this really is the person with whom you want to have a committed relationship; and, if so,
- maintain the love and intimacy in the long-term.

Don't just read about it – do it!

This book needs to be used, not just read; merely reading it will not change your life! It is full of practical exercises designed to give you insight into yourself and, empowered with this self-awareness, to open up opportunities for you to do things differently. .

Making a commitment to marry or to be with someone for the long-term is an important decision that warrants a lot of consideration – it is also hugely exciting. Among the areas we cover is how to introduce more fun and variety into your relationships and your life as a whole. We'll explore things like sexual chemistry and love at first sight, and how sometimes we let our loins rule our head and heart and, consequently, our behaviour.

This book is about hope, encouragement and possibilities; it is also about moving forward and letting go. It's about courage, too, because we're going to be asking you to be very honest and straight with yourself, so that you can set out from a place of maximum awareness.

We're not just talking about *finding* a partner – there are already plenty of books that tell you how not to be single. We want to go beyond that and help you to find and build a life and a relationship that will inspire and energize you to be your best; a life and a relationship in which you don't compromise your own integrity or sell out on yourself in order to have a partner at all costs. If you follow the path we set out here, you will gain the insight, knowledge and wisdom to know what you really want and hold out for it. And when you have found it, we will also offer you some tools with which to help you to sustain it.

How to use this book

If you want a loving relationship to which you can bring *all* of you and in which you are free fully to express your true self, then completing the exercises and working your way chapter by chapter through the book will help you create a much stronger possibility of making this happen.

Finding and building a positive relationship with another individual requires commitment and, at times, hard work. You may find some of the processes in this book challenging, because we will be asking you to focus on things that you may normally prefer not to look too closely. If you find the prospect a little daunting or you think you might find it hard to stay motivated, you might find it helpful to set up a support group with friends or find someone who is also committed to taking a different approach to finding their mate. Working with another person or a team of people will generate synergy from which you can draw strength. You will also be able to encourage and keep one another on track and accountable for your actions.

Another option is to visit our website *www.therelationshipcafe.com* and find out about our telephone coaching groups, which are facilitated by one of our experienced coaches, or about other means of support that we offer.

We suggest that, having created a level of support that works for you, you work through the book chapter-by-chapter, allowing yourself at least three months to do so. There is a reason for the order of chapters and we would encourage you to follow them in that order. Ideally, read through the book once first, very quickly, just skimming the exercises, so that you can gain an overview before you begin doing the work. Then start again from the beginning.

If you've already done quite a lot of personal development work on yourself you may want to skip a few of the exercises in some of the chapters, but you will also find that many of them are new. Take all the time you need to work through the whole sequence. We would encourage you to do as many of the exercises as possible in order to get the maximum you can from the book. Don't hurry through it – you will benefit most if you give yourself some time to reflect on what you have learned at different points.

If you are currently dating and meeting a variety of people, you might like to simplify things for yourself and take a break from dating for the time being while you work through the first five chapters. Then you will be able to revisit dating with a new level of awareness and renewed enthusiasm, and start practising again using our guide to dating as set out in chapter 6.

If you are already in a relationship and are wondering whether it is the right one for you or how you could improve it, then we're not suggesting a relationship holiday in this case. In fact, you might even want to do some of the exercises with your partner.

For each of you the journey will be different. But it will be a journey chosen by you, and that will make the difference.

We wish you well on your path.

1

Taking Responsibility

Between stimulus and response, there is a space. In that space lies our freedom and power to choose our response. In our response lies our growth and freedom.

From *Man's Search for Meaning* by Viktor Frankl (1905–1997)

We all want to love and be loved; and yet finding love and keeping it alive can seem to be the greatest challenge we face.

Love is the central theme of much of our popular music, our favourite television programmes and films, the novels on our bookshelves, the celebrity magazines – even the daily papers. Every day there seems to be a new headline about the latest celebrity couple to have got together or who are breaking up. Nor is our preoccupation with love just a modern phenomenon. Look at the great works of literature, from Geoffrey Chaucer to William Shakespeare to Ernest Hemingway and all the other great writers in between who write of the search for love, the excitement of love, the loss of love, the joy of love and the heartbreak of love. What can we take from all of this?

The stories we read about or watch unfold on our television and cinema screens are a often merely a reflection of what goes on in our own lives. The stories in our own lives are often the most powerful and shape not only how we view the world, but also how we act and respond to others when in a relationship. Part of what we will do in the following chapters is to help you become aware that this is *your* story and to put you in a position of choice from which you can rewrite it for yourself.

We believe that every single one of us has a need to be intimately and lovingly connected with another. It's part of our make-up as human beings. It's what gets us out of bed in the morning and keeps us going when the going gets tough – and it can also drive us to distraction. Research of extremely happy people by psychologists Diener and Seligman found that every person apart from one in the top ten per cent of the most happy people was either married or in a long-term committed relationship. Marriage and long-term commitment to another was found to be the most powerful factor to happiness, over and above job satisfaction, finances and community. This was also found to be true across all 17 ethnic groups that were included in the study. Nevertheless, we may not always be in touch with that need for love; on the other hand, we may sometimes resort to rather extreme ways to get it met, not all of which are helpful to us.

We want you to realize that in your search for love you are anything but alone. There are hundreds and thousands and millions of us doing the same, which gives you two huge advantages. First, there are lots of people to support you in the process, and second, there is a huge number of people out there for you to choose from. And if this book is about *love* it is also about *choice*. We want to support you in creating more options for yourself so that you are in the position of chooser, rather than waiting to be chosen.

But first, in order that you get the most from this book, it's important to do a bit of preparation by focusing on what it is you want in your life and love relationships. Maybe you have never actually been 'in love' or had a long-term relationship; or perhaps you're one of those people who fall 'in love' easily. Maybe you are recovering after a relationship break-up; or perhaps you feel ready to find someone special, someone you could share your life with. Maybe you just want to meet more people and experiment with relationships a little. Whatever your position, reading these pages is a sign that what you want for your present and future is something a bit different from what you have had and done in the past.

We recommend you start a 'Love Journal'. Choose a special book in which you can record your thoughts and experiences. This will really enhance your learning; it's a great way to work through any confusion that might arise for you and help you achieve greater clarity – and the clearer you are about what you want, the easier it is to create it.

You can also use your journal to record the good things that happen. When we get to a block in anything, we often tend to focus on the negative. If you get to that point, it can be very liberating to look back at just how far you have come, what you have already achieved and what you appreciate about your life and experiences.

Our whole purpose in writing this book is to help you change your present situation. Now, however, comes the challenging part. You could read every page of this book, complete all the exercises – and then return to your life and find nothing had changed. That's because this book on its own will not make a jot of difference with-out four vital ingredients; and all of those ingredients relate to you.

They are:
- responsibility;
- openness;
- focus;
- commitment.

You might say you want a relationship. But at what cost? And how much are you prepared to give of yourself to create the relationship you want? You're going to need all four ingredients to keep you on your journey and there will be times you might find yourself asking, 'Is it really worth it?'

Before we go any further, then, it makes sense to look at each of these ingredients individually and identify what your position is to each of them.

Responsibility

No one can make me feel inferior without my consent.
Eleanor Roosevelt (1884–1962)

How much do you agree with the quotation above? Do you think others can make you behave or feel a certain way? When it comes to loving relationships, what does taking responsibility mean?

Well, you've certainly taken a step in the right direction if you have picked up this book and have decided to do things differently from now on. But where might your thoughts and attitudes show that you have not yet taken responsibility for what happened in your past relationships and the position you are in now?

EXERCISE: HAVE YOU AVOIDED TAKING RESPONSIBILITY?

Take a look at the statements below and, being totally honest with yourself, consider which statements you have ever caught yourself saying:

	Yes	No
You make me so angry!		
All I wanted was for you to love me.		
If it hadn't been for him/her being so disloyal/unloving/bad-tempered (replace with one of your own words) I wouldn't be in this mess now.		
Look how you've hurt me.		
All men are bastards!/All women are money grabbers.		
I can't help it, if you'd had a childhood like mine…		
I'm not going to trust others, I've been let down too often.		
I've resigned myself to a life without a partner.		

Even if you relate to only one of the statements on page 13 – and if you selected only one, then we take our hats off to you! – you have blamed someone or something outside yourself; and when we blame we are not taking responsibility. We are choosing to see ourselves as victims.

The psychological system called 'Transactional Analysis' presents a model called the 'drama triangle' (see below), which shows how we get ourselves into different roles of victim, rescuer and persecutor, each reacting to the others.

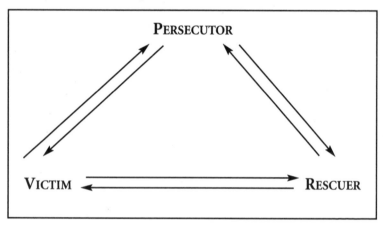

These roles are interchangeable, one minute we may act as victim, wanting someone to rescue us: 'All I want is for you to love me'; but when the love we receive is not what we had in mind, we may become a persecutor who turns on our rescuer accusingly, saying something like 'I think you've turned into an old nag, no wonder nobody listens to you'. This behaviour risks pushing the other person in the relationship into an alternative role and is what is known as a psychological game, which is perpetuated when we are not aware it is happening. Developing awareness of the different roles we can adopt in relationships helps us take responsibility for ourselves and break the patterns of the games we get into.

Some of you may feel justified in taking the victim position. Perhaps you have been abused and seemed to have no control over what happened to you. This will be particularly true if you were abused as a child. Certainly, things can and do happen to us that are out of our control; we didn't ask for them to happen, nor did we ask for the effects they had on us, which can be extremely detrimental. But whatever happened is now in the past. You cannot change the fact that it happened – but you *can* change how you allow it to affect your life in the present and future. We know from our own experiences that while we stay in victim mode and continue to avoid taking responsibility, we perpetuate our sense of helplessness and vulnerability to the power of others.

Suzanne's Story

Suzanne was very unhappily married to a man who was verbally and physically abusive. Over time she lost her confidence and sense of self-worth and became stuck in victim mode. Despite making some attempts to ask her husband to change, she had little impact on his behaviour. 'Poor Suzanne,' her friends would say, 'look at what she has to put up with' – and she agreed with them, blaming her husband and her circumstances for her unhappiness.

Suzanne thought marriage had to be worked at, at all costs, even that of her physical safety and emotional well-being. What she didn't realize was that by accepting her marriage as it was, she wasn't actually working at it but rather tolerating it; and when we tolerate anything, we are not being responsible.

She came to coaching to work on other parts of her life, but understandably her relationship with her husband emerged in her coaching sessions. A breakthrough happened when she realized to her horror that she was providing her children with a totally distorted model of what marriage was like.

With the support of her coach she was able to step back and take a rational view of her past relationships and see how her own behaviour contributed to the abusive patterns in her marriage. While she clearly could not be responsible for her husband's abusive manner, she could be responsible for how she responded and reacted to it.

Suzanne also realized that her own self-worth was greatly influenced by her experiences as a child. She had grown up believing that she was not 'good enough', and she therefore put up with, and at times provoked, her husband's behaviour.

All the time Suzanne remained in victim mode she was rendering herself powerless and giving her power away to others. Once she was able to take responsibility for herself and only herself, she immediately put herself in a position to take some positive and constructive action.

If you were a victim of abuse as a child, when your age, size and developmental level meant that you had no power, it is important that as an adult you step back and recognize that what happened in the past is not your present, nor is it your future. As adults, we have ultimate power over the choices we make and how we wish to conduct our lives. Even if lack of money seems to keep us stuck in an impossible marriage, we still have a decision to make. If we weigh up our options and decide not to leave, that is our choice, albeit not a pleasant one.

Once we take this thought on board and act on it, then we are taking responsibility – and then we can start to create the things we really want in our lives.

EXERCISE: HOW CAN YOU START TAKING RESPONSIBILITY?

Do a quick check for yourself. Reflect on your life as a whole and, in your Love Journal, make a note of any situation in which you might be blaming someone or something else or where you are beating yourself up for your circumstances. What might be your contribution to this situation?

Using the table below as an example, also note in your journal anything you could do to be more actively responsible in the same situation or circumstances.

Areas of my life where I need to take responsibility: how I am contributing to this situation.	What I'm going to do to be more responsible.
I know I am in dire straits financially and have no idea about cash flow. I tend to bury my head in the sand rather than face up to the truth of the situation.	I'm going to learn how to use a financial software programme that will help me track my income and expenses.

The language of responsibility

What we say reflects what is going on for us internally; the words we use reflect our thoughts and feelings. Similarly, the language we use can have a great impact on how powerful we feel.

The phrases that appear in the exercise on page 13 represent what is known as 'victim-type' language: every time we use such phrases we perpetuate to ourselves and others the image of us as a victim.

For example, if you say 'I'm always the one left out at parties' – in other words, I'm a *victim* – this may elicit sympathy from some people. They may want to help you and ask you to join in – this is *rescuing* in the terms of the drama triangle and only helps you to avoid taking responsibility for yourself. On the other hand, people may feel irritated and unsympathetic and tell you to stop moaning, thereby acting out the role of *persecutor*. Either way, communicating from the place of a victim perpetuates the victim position. In both responses the other parties are still in the position of power.

EXERCISE: CHANGING VICTIM LANGUAGE

Have a think about some of your own victim statements. What is it that you catch yourself saying and how could you turn your statements around into more responsible language? We've done a few below to get you started. Note any that are relevant to yourself in your journal.

Victim language	Responsible language
You make me so angry.	I get angry.
All I wanted was for you to love me.	I want love and I'll start by loving myself.
If it hadn't been for him/her being so disloyal/unloving/bad-tempered (replace with one of your own words) I wouldn't be in this mess now.	I cannot control how he/she acts and although I don't like the situation I'm in right now, I will make sure I don't get into it again.
Look how you've hurt me.	I feel hurt about what's happened between us.

Handling the truth about our lives

ARIANA'S STORY: There's a saying, 'the present is happening perfectly'. Now, when my marriage was on the verge of breaking up and somebody said that to me, I reacted angrily, because nothing seemed to be happening perfectly at all.

And yet I knew that, as someone who believes in the concept of personal responsibility, I had to give some consideration to exactly what it was that was happening so perfectly, because it didn't seem obvious. And of course it was perfect (although not very pleasant), because my whole life and all the experiences and wisdom I had drawn from it had led me to a present that was just how it was and exactly how it should be.

I had known for a long time, although I'd been too frightened to admit it, that my marriage was not working and that I had been denying a part of myself while I remained in it. It was almost as if I had become two people within the marriage, my inner self not matching up with the woman on the outside. I had been trying too long to be the woman I knew my husband wanted me to be. But I was not that person and the pretence had become a struggle to sustain, at a cost to both my mental and physical well-being.

I had sold out on myself when I married my husband, despite the fact that I adored him; in truth, I had known it at the time but was not brave enough to back out. But I was not going to do it again. I knew that the present truly was happening perfectly and that I was in control of my response to it.

Up until that point I had allowed myself to be a victim of my circumstances; by finally facing the truth about my life and taking responsibility for it, I had taken the first steps in empowering myself.

EXERCISE: HANDLING THE TRUTH ABOUT OUR LIVES

In your journal, note your answers to the following questions. The first question in this exercise may require you to do some soul-searching. Maybe you need to ask a friend what truth they think you might be avoiding. This is a tough one. And the best way to avoid facing the truth is not to ask yourself the question in the first place. How honest do you think you can be with yourself?

- Is there a truth you need to face up to in your life that you are avoiding? Can you name it?
- How much are you truly yourself in your life?
- How much are you truly yourself in your relationships?
- What are the short-term gains that might be stopping you from facing up to this truth?
- What are the long-term consequences of not facing up to this truth?

Openness

Chance favours only the open mind.

Anon.

The second ingredient that we believe is important in order for you to get the most out of this book and to create more loving relationships in your life is openness: a receptive, curious outlook and curiosity rather than defensiveness, cynicism, scepticism and tunnel vision. How open do you think you are? Both of us have had times in our lives when we have thought we were very open and it has been a surprise for us to realize that actually we were less so than we thought.

So, how open do you think you are? How often while reading the pages of this book have you caught yourself questioning the validity of what we might be saying? How often have you thought to yourself that this is all well and good in theory or in an idealized world, but the real world is not the same? Or have you found yourself being receptive to some of the ideas we've been talking about? Perhaps you've even started to imagine how you might like things to be for you?

Do you tend to have the sceptic's attitude of been there, done that, got the T-shirt and maybe have the scars to prove it? Or do you accept that there might be an alternative view by staying curious and asking questions, allowing yourself to remain open to the answers that come up?

So let's look at what we mean by scepticism. The sceptic's reluctance to accept what they are told usually develops from a painful past experience. In order to protect ourselves from further hurt, we become critical and doubting. You don't usually see young children being sceptical: life is full of adventure and fun for them; they naïvely throw themselves into every experience and learn from it. But as we grow up we learn to distinguish between good and bad, joy and pain; and where we've experienced some pain, we put in place a defence in order to avoid experiencing it again.

As with responsibility, our scepticism often shows up in the way we speak to ourselves or to others. And the reason we're bringing it to your attention is that what scepticism does is keep you safe, because it stops you from taking risks. But for the same reason it also keeps you stuck. If you have questioned the validity of what you have read here so far, we would like to make a few suggestions.

- **First, suspend judgement.** We often quickly jump into judging others, and all that serves to do is to limit how we are with that person and how we allow them to be with us.
- **Secondly, be curious.** What other options might be available to you? Could there be another way of looking at the same situation? Could there be another way of handling it?
- **Thirdly, lighten up.** Scepticism is driven by insecurity and fear of being hurt; the more you can get outside yourself, go with what is around you and have fun, the more you will open yourself up to learning and receiving some of the positive things that are available.

Focus

We're now at the stage where we'd like you to focus – to think about what it is you really want and set some compelling goals for yourself.

Often when we set goals we write them down and then put them in a drawer and forget about them. Perhaps it's because, although we think we would like to achieve the goal, or we should achieve it, in fact it doesn't really excite us or capture our imagination. The result is that we don't possess the energy or motivation to pursue it to the end.

Whatever may have happened in the past, this is your chance to start creating the kind of relationship you really want – to set a realistic goal for yourself that will excite and energize you.

If you're not in a relationship now, you have some valuable space to explore what it is you want. The clearer and more excited you are about this, the more likely you are to achieve it.

If you are in a relationship, maybe there are things you'd like to be different. We're not talking about changing your partner – indeed, you might wish to ask him or her to engage in this process with you so that you can create some joint goals for how you would like your relationship to be.

EXERCISE: SETTING A COMPELLING GOAL FOR YOURSELF

What is your purpose in reading this book? Think about it.

You might say 'I want a relationship' or 'I want my relationship to be different' – but what sort of relationship do you want, or how do you want it to be different? It's important to get specific now. Write your goal in your journal.

You might like to check your language. Does your goal take you away from your current situation, for example, 'I don't want to be single any more'? If it does, the emphasis is still on being single; that is what you will continue to think about, and so that is how you are likely to remain. In other words, make your goal something you can move *towards*. Make it a really positive vision of what you want, not just an escape from your current circumstances.

It's impossible to emphasize enough how powerful language can be. If we say to you, 'Don't think of a green elephant', what do you automatically think of? You're probably already thinking about that green elephant. So if you have written something that is negative, it is quite likely to take you towards what it is you *don't* want.

Think about it. When we say to ourselves, 'I must not eat unhealthy food', what do we start thinking about? And of course, as we keep thinking about all those chocolates, cakes and fries, the more likely we are to break our resolve and tuck in. Similarly, the more we think, 'I don't want someone to take me for granted', then the more likely we are to end up with just that.

So make sure you have stated your goal in positive terms – and in the present tense, so that it really has force. For example: 'I have someone in my life who appreciates and values me'.

Now build up a picture of this goal. Make it really vivid and colourful. What are you noticing, what are you seeing around you, what are you hearing people saying, what are you feeling? How would others know that you have achieved your goal? Write it out in your journal.

Do you now have a goal that is energizing and exciting for you and that gives you a really clear picture of what you want? If so, make achieving this your clear and positive intention. Know that you can get to your goal – provided you give yourself a good dollop of the fourth ingredient: commitment.

Commitment

A man was walking along a beach one day and saw that hundreds of starfish had been washed up on the shore. He saw a woman bending and picking up the starfish and throwing them back into the sea. The beach unfolded ahead of him and seemed to go on for ever. He walked across to the woman and asked, 'Why are you throwing the starfish back into the sea?' The woman replied, 'The sun is up. It will soon be hot and the starfish will dry out and die. I'm throwing them back so they might live.' 'But', said the man, 'what is the point? You will never save all of them. The beach goes on for ever and you can never make a difference.' The woman picked up another fish, threw it into the cool waves and said: 'I've just made a difference to that one, haven't I?'

Anon.

The immediate point of this story is to show how just one small step at a time can make a difference, because, sometimes, as with the beach and all the starfish on it, our task can seem never-ending and laborious; it can be hard to see if we are making any difference at all. But every step, no matter how small, does matter. Even if we can't immediately see the effects, we will be making a difference. As with a child learning to walk, just a few steps each day allows the child to consolidate the learning and to go a few steps further forward the next day and the next. Such learning takes dogged determination and commitment.

So, too, with our lives. Except now it gets harder, because, in a sense, we're undoing all the old learnings, as well as finding new ways of stepping forward. And to expect things to change overnight when we've been doing them the same way for 20, 30, 40 years or more, is unrealistic. It will take time.

However, as with the starfish, even one change, albeit tiny, will make a difference, which will have a snowball effect as it gathers momentum. As you begin to change, the people around you will begin to respond to you in different ways. This is all the more reason for you to take it slowly, to allow time to integrate the new learnings so that they become truly a part of you at what is known as a cellular level. Once the new learnings become integrated at this level you will have them for life.

So, how committed are you to changing things for yourself? Will you leaf through this book, think there are some nice ideas and then put it down? Or will you actually follow the suggestions and take some action that will make a difference to you?

One thing is for sure: commitment is about taking action, and not just half-hearted action, but action with the full intention of doing something different.

This immediately brings up the issue of fear. Making a commitment and taking action can be scary. After all, doing what we've always done has meant we've survived to tell our story today; maybe if we do something different we might rock the boat too much.

But think. Are you going to be taking any action that is life-threatening to you? Probably not. So try thinking about it this way – you just can't fail. For, at the very least, you will be learning something about yourself that will equip you better for whatever the future holds.

EXERCISE: HOW COMMITTED ARE YOU?

Think about your level of commitment to this process. Look back at the goal you wrote in your journal for the exercise on page 21 and below it note your answers to the following questions:

- Is what you have written really important to you?
- To what degree are you prepared to step out of your comfort zone to achieve what you want?
- How much are you choosing this area of your life for yourself and how much to gain approval from others?
- What will achieving your goal do for you?
- Is this important enough to keep you going, despite the hurdles that you might have to face along the way?
- Who or what did you allow to get in your way when you tried to create a similar change in the past?
- What are you prepared to do to ensure you don't allow this to happen again?
- On a scale of 1 to 10, to what degree are you willing to turn the page on your past and do things differently? Mark your answer below.

Unwilling					Totally willing				
1	2	3	4	5	6	7	8	9	10

- On a scale of 1 to 10, to what extent are you prepared to take responsibility for the fact that it is you that needs to change to achieve what you want and not others? Mark your answer below.

I think it is others that need to change					It's all up to me				
1	2	3	4	5	6	7	8	9	10

Reflect on your answers and consider how honest you've been. There's no point kidding yourself at this stage, unless you want to convince yourself that 'nothing works'.

Are you prepared to take the time to read this book thoroughly and do the exercises seriously? The extent to which you are prepared to make this commitment to yourself will have a massive influence on the whole of the rest of your life. But if you just read it and don't do the exercises, then not a lot will change. The key word is the one we have chosen for the chapter title: responsibility. And it's you who have to take that responsibility.

Time to get going!

We hope now that you know exactly what your goal is in reading this book, that you are prepared to take responsibility for your own life, to be open to possibility and to commit yourself to treading the path that will take you towards the kind of relationship you deserve – a relationship in which you feel free to be yourself, which energizes and supports you to be your best and in which you find the two-way connection that having a soulmate can offer you – without surrendering your soul to achieve it.

Dare to go for what you are truly worth. Stay committed to yourself first and foremost. As the great German poet and scholar Goethe (1749–1832) said:

Until one is committed, there is hesitancy, the chance to draw back, always ineffectiveness concerning all acts of initiative and creation. Whatever you can do or dream you can, begin it. Boldness has genius, power and magic in it. Begin it now.

2

Clearing Your Clutter

If it ain't broke... make it better.

From *Loving What Is* by Byron Katie

Now that you have some clear goals for what you want to achieve with regard to bringing more love into your life, the first step is to get ready for it. In this chapter you will learn to let go of messages, feelings and memories from your past that may hamper you in reacting and responding to situations and people now.

This chapter will help you discover more about yourself in relation to your past and look at what may be getting in the way of the life you want to have. In gaining more understanding of who you are, as opposed to who others have expected you to be, you will give yourself a choice between carrying on as before or moving into a different way of being.

By the end of this chapter we hope you will have begun to:

- understand what role models and beliefs you have absorbed from your childhood experiences and what impact these have had on your life up until now;

- recognize what you are holding on to from past relationships (both with your parents and with previous partners) and how this may affect your emotions and behaviour in the present;

- appreciate why knowing yourself better and becoming aware of the patterns you have recreated in your life will help you choose a partner who is right for you;

- identify some practical things you can do to let go of unhelpful beliefs so that you can be clear to enter a new relationship.

Healing and letting go of what has happened before, realizing that your present and future don't have to be like your past, can transform your life. As well as giving you more positive energy and a sense of self-worth, your renewed energy will make you far more attractive – so you can win on all sides if you're committed to doing this work.

At times, it's true, this work can be challenging: things might come up that you find uncomfortable, even painful. If you are concerned about this, then please do seek support, either from a sympathetic friend or from a coach or therapist.

How did your childhood influence you?

Whatever your childhood was like, you will have absorbed certain beliefs, attitudes and values as a direct result of how you were brought up, and many of these will have been superimposed onto the relationships you have formed since, right up to the present. Thirty years ago or more, it was rare for your classmates not to have both their parents living at home. Today, there is a whole generation of children whose parents have divorced and many fear making the same mistakes. Gay couples are having children. Our role models have changed and what was once considered the norm has now changed beyond recognition. Over the following pages we will be asking you to question some of the messages that you picked up during your upbringing and consider how these might be helping or hindering you in the relationships you make in your life now.

What would your life be like now if you were living according to the very same rules that your parents grew up with? Are most of those rules still relevant? Probably not. Times and attitudes change, and what worked half a century or more ago may simply not fit these days.

Each of us has individual and unique experiences not only in our families of origin, but also in our schools and our communities. All shape and influence how we act, think and feel. Some of these influences may have empowered us, but just as many of them will have constrained us and placed us in our own psychic prisons.

Jenny's Story

Jenny asked her father why she had she been hit as a child. His answer was that it had worked for him, so there was no reason why it should not have worked for her too. He had been a fighter pilot during the Second World War and she has no doubt that his disciplined childhood training worked wonders for him in the armed forces, where life is governed by rules and regulations.

But such discipline hadn't worked for her – indeed, she is convinced that it could not have, unless she had wanted to follow a similar career path to that of her father. She became the archetypal 'good child'. Her upbringing was strict, but not altogether unhappy. She never sought to question that there might be another way, another viewpoint; she just thought that that was how it was. Her parents' views on life were her views. Their anxieties became her anxieties. Their values were her values. Thus it became easier to toe the line and not upset anyone along the way.

Some of us will have been 'good children'. Others will have rebelled against our upbringing and gone completely the opposite way, determined not to be like our parents or influenced by them. Whether we seek our parents' approval or purposely decide to rebel against them, like it or not we are still allowing them to influence us, and this can get in our way and results in us behaving in ways that aren't actually very useful to us.

Why do we need to know all this?

So long as we have not separated what might have been true for our parents, but is no longer true for us, from what is genuinely important for ourselves, we are not really in control of our lives, although we may think we are. While we continue to make our decisions on the basis of past conditioning, we are living according to beliefs and standards passed down to us by previous generations, attitudes we have not chosen for ourselves. We are not our parents.

When you begin to reflect on the conditioning you have received from your childhood, and look at how your past might be affecting your present, you may feel reluctant to go down this route for fear of seeming disloyal to those you love. But remember that therapy, coaching and the whole field of personal development was not so widely available to earlier generations as it is to us now; there is no disloyalty in taking advantage of new opportunities for self-awareness that were simply not open to our parents and grandparents.

And with awareness comes change and the possibility of improvement. What we are aiming to do in this book is not just to enable you to gain insight and awareness, but also to give you the tools to equip you to choose and create something new and wonderful for yourselves.

Your map of the world

We absorb messages as children and often never question their validity, even as adults. They form part of our personal 'map' of the world and shape our beliefs and values, both those by which we judge other situations and people, and those that dictate how we feel about ourselves. One of the messages Ariana received from her father was that men are not attracted to successful women. How do you think might that have affected her approach to her career?

The following exercises are designed to get you to look at your own map of the world and to notice what rules you are living your life by. Are these rules still working for you? If not, maybe it's time to let them go. We want you to notice the family stories that you have taken on board as your own, even though they may no longer be valid for you. What are these stories and how are they defining your life?

EXERCISE: MESSAGES FROM CHILDHOOD

Tick any of the sentences in the exercise box on the following page that may ring true for you and add any others that apply to you and are not included.

If you were to accept that many of these messages relate only to your own family's view of life, are untrue and may well be unhelpful as a basis for your life, which ones would you want to begin to let go of? What new messages would you want to create for yourself instead?

	Yes	No
It's rude to talk about money.		
It's not OK to express feelings in our family.		
He who shouts loudest gets the most attention.		
If you're a girl, looks count more than brains.		
Work comes before pleasure.		
I wish you'd been a boy.		
He's the bright one in the family.		
Anything fun is immoral, illegal or fattening.		
Marry for money, not love.		
Women should look after the home.		
Women don't really enjoy sex but only do it to keep a man happy.		
Boys don't cry.		
I wish you'd been a girl.		
We must always be nice to each other.		
Don't get angry.		
I'll tell you what to do, you're opinion doesn't count.		
Look what I'm giving up for you.		
Be good and I'll love you more.		
You are second best.		
You are not enough.		
Achievement is everything.		
Add others:		

The 'normal' family

Most of us grow up believing that our family is just the same as everybody else's. So if we grow up in a family of two-point-four kids, hardly ever seeing our father because he's separated from our Mum, or if we grow up in the care of childminders or having to fend for ourselves after school because our Mum's working five days a week that seems perfectly normal, until we get much older. In fact, it might remain 'normal' for the rest of our lives, as we will have certain expectations when it comes to starting our own families.

We will all have had our own unique experiences of family life. How might these different backgrounds colour our expectations, and what effect might that have on the partners we choose and on the way we manage our lives?

Our own positioning within the family will also have influenced some of our attitudes to life and love. Depending upon whether we were the eldest child, the youngest or somewhere in the middle, an only child or one of several, we will each have a different perspective of what it was like to be a member of a family group, and this will have some bearing on our experiences as an adult.

The purpose of the next exercise is to make you more aware of what was considered normal in your home. You will then be in a position to reflect on how much of this is still relevant for you, whether it suits the kind of relationships you would like to have in your life, and what you might like to change.

EXERCISE: YOUR ROLE AND POSITION IN YOUR FAMILY OF ORIGIN

In your journal note down your answers to the following questions:

- What roles did your parents assume when you were growing up? And were there gender differences?
- What was each of your parents like (personality, behaviour, etc.)?
- What was your parents' relationship with each other like?
- How did they demonstrate love for each other?
- What was their relationship with you like?

- How did they demonstrate love to to you?
- Who had more influence over you?
- How do you think being the oldest, youngest, etc. affected you?
- How did your family describe you?
- What was your role in the family (e.g. the baby/the carer)?
- What was expected of you?
- What did you expect?
- How did you experience love overall?
- What bearing does all this have on your experiences and expectations of adult couple relationships?

Having reviewed your experiences within the family:

- What do you think are the key themes and messages that come through for you?
- How do they empower or limit you?
- How are you perpetuating these messages in your life now?
- Thinking of the messages you'd like to change, what would be the smallest thing you could do that would make the biggest difference to you?

Take a look at Angela's story.

Angela's Story

Angela came with trepidation to one of our workshops. She was tall and elegantly dressed with a pretty face; you should have been able to describe her as a woman with presence, and yet somehow she did not leave any impression at all. She kept her head low and rounded her shoulders. It was almost as though she were invisible.

During an exercise where similar questions were asked to those above; Angela realized that, as the middle child of three, quite often she used to disappear and nobody would notice that she had gone.

Her family used to call her the elusive one and she lived up to that label. At school, she used to disappear during breaks and nobody really noticed that she had gone. And in our workshop, the sense of her being invisible seemed to fit. It was almost as though she didn't feel she had a right to be there; it was as if she was doing the ostrich act of sticking her head in the sand. By pretending not to be there, by not being fully present, she felt safer somehow.

She had recently come out of a six-year relationship with someone who had three children. When they were all together as a family, she often felt as if she did not really exist. The children would clamour for attention from their father, whom they only saw at weekends, and hardly noticed Angela. She would escape from the house, saddle her horse and go off riding for a couple of hours. She knew that it was unlikely that anyone would notice her absence.

Angela was shocked when she began to acknowledge the pattern she had been following throughout most of her life. By the end of the workshop she was beginning to stand taller and more confidently, and was able to look people in the eyes knowing that she, too, had a right to be there and had something worthwhile to contribute.

Beliefs and assumptions

So far we've looked at your childhood experiences, the role models in your life and the messages that were passed on to you, all of which contribute to the set of personal beliefs that we develop. By the time children are three years old they are already in possession of their own well-formed sets of beliefs, so we are talking about a structure that we've been buying into for a fairly long time.

Beliefs are the thoughts we hold that shape our reality and they are often demonstrated through the assumptions we make about ourselves and about others. Did you believe in Father Christmas when you were a child? How did that show in your feelings and behaviour? What did you do to perpetuate the belief and make your reality match it? For example, did you hang up your stocking, leave a mince pie out for Father Christmas and a carrot for his reindeer?

Strongly held beliefs have a very powerful influence over us, helping us to make sense of what is happening in our world; and, of course, we all believe that our beliefs are the only ones that are really true! The fact that we create our own reality or truth through our beliefs and continue to find evidence to prove to ourselves that we are right means not only that our beliefs influence what we create for ourselves, but that they can result in our resisting any kind of change. Our beliefs give us security, keep us safe, stop us raising the bar or stepping out of our comfort zone.

Yet beliefs are no more than powerful thoughts that we have formed on the basis of our past. They may have served us then, but they might not serve us now. We need to learn that there is not just one truth: there are many truths, all of which might apply to any one of us.

We can usually recognize our beliefs in our language. Whenever you catch yourself saying 'I should…', 'I must…', 'I have to…', you are expressing a belief. What's important is to start recognizing the ones that support you and the ones that limit you.

EXERCISE: SHED THE SHOULDS, THE HAVE-TOS AND THE MUSTS

This exercise is designed to encourage you to identify the beliefs you hold about relationships specifically and to see where they are holding you back. For each of the beliefs in the first column of the table on the opposite page, ask yourself:

- Does this belief empower or limit me?
- Who says I must believe this?
- What's the evidence to support the belief?
- Do I want or choose to change this?

If your answer to the last question is 'yes', then rewrite the belief in the second column, changing the statement into one that empowers you. We've done the first couple to get you started.

If you have some beliefs that are absolutely not serving you well, what can you do about them? Well, you can take each belief individually and dissect it in stages. We've started you off with an example. Record the answers to your own beliefs in your journal.

1. **What is a major belief you hold about yourself that stops you from propelling yourself forward to create the life you want?**
   For example: There are very few suitable single men/women available.

Shoulds, have-tos and musts	Wants/choices
I must keep the home nice.	I choose to take care of my home and share the responsibility.
I have to be the breadwinner.	I want to contribute to my family's livelihood.
I'm a woman, therefore I shouldn't make the first move.	
I have to be strong to be masculine.	
I shouldn't be too assertive because it's not feminine.	
I should try to be as witty and eloquent as other people.	
I must always look good.	
I have to be in charge.	
I shouldn't tell someone I like them, even when I do.	
I should wait for them to call me.	
In your journal, add some of your own.	

2. **How does this belief that you're holding right now protect you?**
   For example: I don't have to make much effort and step outside my comfort zone if I don't believe there are any men/women available.

3. **How is having this belief unhelpful for you?**
   For example: I've given up on making the best of myself and going out socially. I stay at home and watch TV a lot.

4. **What evidence do you have that the belief is true?**

5. **What could be the real truth here? (Make this the opposite of the belief you had in question 1).**

6. Here comes the powerful bit – if you were to choose to act as if the opposite to your original belief were true, what would change for you? How would your life and your relationships be different?
   No examples here. This is for you to work out.

7. So what's stopping you from making this choice?

Relationship patterns

It seems so simple. Your eyes meet across a crowded room, you smile at one another, you spend the whole evening talking, you arrange to meet again – and before long you're feeling whole, fully alive and connected, as if you have known each other since time immemorial. You are in love, and you *know* you were meant to be together for ever!

So how come what starts out in such a promising way so often does not have a happy ending? It's intriguing that, despite the despair we may feel when we are stuck in a loveless relationship (which in most cases did not start that way) and the grief we experience when a relationship breaks down, we still keep bouncing back optimistically, ready to believe that if we could only find our one true love we would be happy.

And yet the divorce statistics suggest that second and third marriages are no more successful than first marriages. What happens? Where do we go wrong?

Well, there are lots of reasons for relationship breakdown, but one useful approach is to ask why we end up with the partners we do. Have you thought that there might be a pattern to the types of love partners that you attract? Coming to understand your relationship patterns will enable you to understand more about your own unfulfilled needs from childhood, and how, perhaps without realizing it, you may be seeking a partner who will meet them.

If you are single, you can decide whether or not these patterns are working for you and what you might want to change. If you are already in a relationship, then this is your wake-up call: because in a long-term, committed relationship, romantic love (based on sexual chemistry and initial attraction) will at some point come to an end –

and at that point a struggle of some kind may emerge, particularly if we begin to realize that the relationship is not meeting all our needs.

Many people fail to recognize their own part in relationship breakdown and are quick to blame their partners, simply moving on to a new relationship where they often repeat the same mistakes because they have not gained the insight or awareness to do things differently. Others may have countless hours of therapy in the hope that they might form successful relationships in the future – and then use this as an intellectual exercise to avoid doing anything about ever becoming really close again. Because, in many respects, staying single can feel safe; it's a great way of avoiding the pain and conflict that can arise through the closeness of an intimate relationship. But is that what you really want?

According to Harville Hendrix, author of *Keeping the Love You Find*, it is not until we are actually in a relationship that the true healing begins. Intimate relationships, more than any other, can press our buttons and flip us right back into old childhood feelings of hurt and anger when it feels like our partner is not meeting our emotional needs.

Relationships offer us the chance to heal the emotional wounds of our childhood, because when we fall in love, we are unconsciously attracted to partners who carry many of the traits – both good and bad – of our parents, in particular (although not always) those of our opposite-sex parent. So when we meet someone and say 'I feel like I've known you all my life', on one level this is actually true, because the feelings and experiences they evoke are reflections of our past early relationships.

Yvonne's and Gary's Story

Yvonne was a successful solicitor and a single mum with children, who lived in a beautiful home. When she came to coaching, the one thing that she felt was missing in her life was someone who would really cherish her.

When she met Gary, it seemed as though her happiness was complete. He adored her and needed her. He had come through a particularly difficult divorce and had been left to cope single-handedly with his three children. He worked long hours for little money.

Gary fulfilled Yvonne's need to rescue and she encouraged him to give up his job so they could move in together. She knew that she was in a position to support Gary and his children financially while he took the chance to sort himself out and decide what his next career move would be.

Merging two families brought its own set of challenges and, invevitably, there were arguments before long. Through coaching, Yvonne began to realize that she had fallen in love with someone who reminded her so much of her own father, a man she had adored, but who had not been able to stand up to his dominant wife. She began to understand why, when Gary's children forgot his birthday, she had wept for him. It was like she was weeping for her own father and repeating a pattern from that past relationship.

Gary's pattern was that he was attracted to women who appeared to be strong, only to find that their apparent emotional strength was just an illusion. He had had close relationships with both his parents, but his mother was undoubtedly the driving force. He had allowed Yvonne to rescue him because he unwittingly sought to recreate the dynamics of his relationship with his mother through his relationships with his partners.

As Yvonne and Gary began to understand more and more how they had chosen each other not only conciously but also at an unconscious level, they learned to let go of the underlying need to recreate the old patterns. As the coaching progressed and they began to trust each other more, Yvonne learned to let go of the need to 'fix' Gary and felt more able to show her vulnerable side, asking for help rather than getting stressed through trying to do everything on her own. Gary learned to accept Yvonne's vulnerability and to support her in times of need.

It was particularly important for Gary not to feel overtaken by Yvonne's desire to help him, and for him to learn to recognize and assert himself. They both learned to express feelings, not only of love and joy but of sadness, frustration or anger, without fear for the relationship. They each began to feel genuinely acknowledged and heard by the other, and the foundation of their relationship became stronger and more united. This, in turn, had a positive effect on the children.

Understanding your relationship patterns will help you to understand yourself better. And greater knowledge of yourself gives you greater freedom as you begin to make more informed choices about how you live and love; freedom to start doing things differently.

EXERCISE: RELATIONSHIP PATTERNS

This exercise will help you to become more consciously aware of what has caused you to make the relationship choices you have made in the past – even if you thought it was just the chemistry! It is a really significant exercise, so allow yourself plenty of time to think about it before you write your answers.

1. **Remember the people who brought you up or who had the most influence over you when you were a child. Draw a line down the middle of a page in your journal, put a '+' sign on the one side and a '–' sign on the other and then, for each of them, answer the following questions.**
- What were they like? Thinking about their personalities and behaviour, list their positive qualities and their negative traits under the plus and minus signs.
- How did they relate to each other? What was good and what was bad?
- How did they relate to you? What was good? What was bad?

2. **Now think about your previous significant relationships.**
- List the qualities, personality traits and behaviours of your previous partners in positive and negative terms.
- How did they relate to you? What was good? What was bad?

3. **Marking the positives and the negatives in different colours, high-light the characteristics that seem to be repeating themselves most often and make a summary list of these.**

4. **What conclusions are you able to draw from your summary list of positives and negatives? What seem to be some of the themes that keep repeating themselves in your relationships? Here are some questions to guide you:**
- What characteristics of your parents have you found in your partners?
- Are you repeating your parents' relationship pattern in your own relationships? How?

- When a partner hurts your feelings, how do you react? Do you punish them? If so, how? In what way do your hurt feelings today remind you of how you felt hurt as a child?
- What else do you notice?

You may feel that you are being disloyal to your parents in the first part of the exercise. Many of us feel this way. But remember that most of our parents did the best that they could with the knowledge, self-awareness and personal resources they possessed at the time.

With this in mind, be honest with yourself and recognize both the positive and negative influences your parents will have had over who you are today and over some of the beliefs that you carry around with you. It's not disloyal to accept that your parents were not perfect; you can acknowledge that they did the best they could, even if your experience of their best might not always have felt that great.

Facing up to the bad times from your childhood and your parents' involvement in this is the first step towards making the personal changes you want to make. Once you have this awareness you are in a position to begin to let go of the feelings, thoughts and behaviours that are no longer helping you. You can then start truly loving your parents, not from a place of childhood duty, but as a free-thinking adult who is able to respond to them equally as adults.

Doing this exercise may well have brought up old memories about which you feel sad, angry or resentful. You might find, also, that you are holding on to old emotions from a more recent relationship. Both will be influencing how you think, feel and behave in the present.

Graham's Story

Graham did the 'Relationship Patterns' exercise after he had been in coaching for a couple of months. He was a cheerful, down-to-earth man in his late 30s who had recently started a new job, which he was thoroughly enjoying. He felt ready to settle down and find a partner; perhaps get married and have children. Yet he felt a certain unease about the relationships that he had had in the past. He knew that he had found it difficult to get really close to anybody and had a sense of trying to run away as soon as he was in a relationship.

Graham's parents had always had a strong influence in his life and, when he first began coaching, he was keen to point out how happy his childhood had been – which undoubtedly it was, for much of the time. But he needed to let go of the 'dutiful son' script that he was following.

He felt uneasy about looking deeper into what was going on in his family. However, he gradually began to admit that his mother was quite domineering. She liked to be right about everything and tended to organize everybody. His father was a gentler person, but could be stubborn. He would often try to escape to the shed at the bottom of the garden, and ultimately would tend to give in rather than get into any kind of conflict.

As Graham did the exercise he began to realize that his past girlfriends had been similar to his mother, and that he had tended, like his father, to opt for a quiet life rather than assert his own needs. His girlfriends always tended to take advantage of his gentle nature and he was aware of vague feelings of discontent; although he hadn't been able to articulate them at the time, he realized that it had been almost as if he was becoming a non-person. When these relationships came to an end, he noticed that he would start to get his old personality back and would feel a lot happier.

It was liberating for Graham to become more consciously aware of the patterns he was repeating and, as the coaching progressed and he began to get a clearer picture of what was important for him, he was able to be more assertive about his own needs. He found that he started to attract a different kind of woman into his life: one who did not try to organize him or change him, but who was able to accept and respect him for the lovely person he was.

Whose life are you living?

Before we leave this theme of relationship patterns, just take a moment to consider the other ways in which your parents or other people from your past may still be influencing your choice of partner. Perhaps you don't want to do anything to risk disappointing them or hurting their feelings. Or perhaps you have decided to rebel against your upbringing and to go for precisely the opposite of what you know they would want.

EXERCISE: WHOSE LIFE ARE YOU LIVING?

Ask yourself the following questions and note you answers in your journal:

- Do you still feel that your parents would have to approve of your partner choice?
- Conversely, are you attracted to potential partners of whom you know your parents would not approve?
- How much are you living up to other people's expectations of you?
- How much do you give up on yourself in order to be loved?

Sally's Story

As a child, Sally was a well-behaved young girl. Her parents were quite strict with her and, as she used to assume that other families all worked the same way, she could never understand why some parents seemed to have no control over the behaviour of their children. Sally knew exactly when she was doing something wrong: her parents only needed to say something in a certain tone of voice and that was enough to stop her in her tracks and make sure she did not upset them. She was very respectful of them and obedient.

Sally grew up to be an attractive woman, but she lacked confidence in her own abilities. She continued to be the archetypal 'good child': she was careful not to have any strong opinions in front of people, as she never wanted to cause offence. In fact, she was not quite sure if she even had any opinions of her own. She just knew it felt a bit scary to articulate her own feelings and preferred to go along with everyone else.

She married a man whom her parents totally approved of and, when they started a family, she was determined to be strict with her children in the same way her parents had been with her. She too believed that children had to behave at whatever cost. She started to feel confused when her young son, instead of conforming, as she would have done, started to rebel at home and at school. She could hear her mother's voice in her as she warned him when he misbehaved or made him feel guilty for causing her extra work.

It was at the age of 31, when her marriage broke up and her son chose to live with her former husband instead of with her, that Sally decided to seek coaching. She realized that she was not living her own life; she was still in the shadow of her parents. She had no real sense of her own identity or of what she believed to be true about the world. All she knew was how to conform to other people's expectation of her.

Letting go

Some of us move from one relationship to another without allowing ourselves the time to get over what happened in our previous relationship, only to find similar issues arising again in the new one. Others feel that they have worked through any residual feeling and are ready to meet someone again, but don't seem able to attract anyone into their lives.

Both of these situations suggest that there are things we might be holding on to from previous relationships that are not helping us in the present. It is therefore really important to work through and let go of emotions connected with our past so that we can be fully open to the present.

MARY'S STORY: In my early 30s I ended a long-term meaningful relationship because I felt I was not doing myself any favours by staying and was feeling increasingly angry and resentful about the circumstances surrounding it. I felt hugely relieved when it was over and went on a social whirl of meeting other people. Yet despite my new-found confidence no one new seemed to be coming into my life. It was almost as if I were wearing an invisible badge that said 'get lost' on it.

Discussing this with my friends, I realized I was still feeling really angry and accusatory about what had happened in my previous relationship. Although my intention was to go out and meet people, I had unconsciously been sending out unfriendly signals.

EXERCISE: WHAT BADGE ARE YOU WEARING?

Think about what you might be carrying from the past and how it might affect the way you are with other people in the present.

- What old hurts from the past might be affecting how you are now?
- What invisible badge might you still be wearing?
- What badge would you really like to be wearing?
- What do you need to let go of to change what is written on your badge?

Letting go can take various forms. Take a look at the list below and see what is the most appropriate method for your circumstances. Emotions can be overwhelming and this can be frightening for us to have to deal with. If this is the case for you, then you may wish to look at the list of resources at the back of this book and select one that suits your needs to get more support in doing this.

- **Write a letter**
  Write a letter to the person with whom you wish to clear your past. This could be a parent, a friend, an old lover, a brother or sister. Write it from the heart: pour out all the things you wanted to say but never did. You don't have to send the letter, just writing it can be enough. You may want to read it to an understanding friend or you could burn it to symbolize your letting go of the past.
- **Make that phone call**
  If there's someone you have been holding yourself back from apologizing to, acknowledging or forgiving – ring them.
- **Talk to an empty chair**
  Imagine the person who is still haunting you is sitting in a chair in front of you and tell them how you really feel – allow yourself to get really emotional.
- **Let the anger out**
  Close the doors and windows so others can't hear you, get a pile of cushions and scream and punch out your anger until you feel better.
- **Re-frame your experience**
  Sometimes experiences we remember as negative can actually help us in ways we haven't yet thought of. By taking another look at the situation or by changing the filter we put on it we can completely change our memories of it. What might you have learned or have even been the gift in your experience?

MARY'S STORY CONTINUED: I can distinctly remember the day that I let go of all the resentment about this particular past relationship. I was driving along a main road in the countryside: it was a cold spring day, the sun was out and the sky was a clear, crisp blue. I'd just successfully completed a series of workshops and was feeling really good. I began to think about my ex-partner. My forehead clouded and knotted and I knew I was still blaming him.

So I asked myself, what had I got out of this relationship? What had being in the relationship, and with him, done for me?

I quickly realized that we had been hugely sexually attracted to each other; we'd had a great sex life and this was the first relationship I had been in where I had woken up as a fully sexual woman. I suddenly appreciated what a tremendous gift I had been given through that relationship and, in accepting the gift, I was able to let go of the hurt that I'd been holding on to over the previous months.

Free yourself from your life script

Together, our childhood experiences and the beliefs that guide us in reinforcing them can result in what some psychologists call a 'life script'. We've started to look at how you can change these patterns for yourself, but your life script can be very deeply embedded and very strong.

Awareness is key to freeing yourself from the chains your script may wrap round you. Each bit of awareness you gain is like one link cut, and you may well have to persevere for quite a while before you begin to see how you could move and feel without these chains. The thing that's important is to keep going: eventually you'll get the insight you need that will take you forward.

Derek's Story

When Derek was in his mid-20s he lived with Carol, an accountant, who had two children, a boy and a girl, who came to stay at weekends. Derek began to notice that he used to feel sometimes as if he was acting out being a parent – it didn't sound like his own voice that was doing the talking. He could sometimes hear himself taking on what would have been the attitude of his father in similar situations.

One day the little boy broke a lamp and came to find Derek to tell him what happened and ask him for something to clear it up with. He lectured him on the waste of money and said he might just as well clear it up himself otherwise it would probably cause him even more work.

A few years later, after his relationship with Carol had broken up, Derek sought coaching, feeling confused about who he was and what he stood for. His beliefs and values apparently matched those of his parents, but he was not at all sure whether they were what he truly felt. It felt as though the inner and outer parts of himself were in conflict with each other – and no wonder, when how he was behaving (the bit on the outside) did not seem to match how he was feeling on the inside.

He looked back at the episode with his ex-partner's son and remembered it as one of many where he felt as if he had taken on a bit-part in a play, and the only lines he knew were ones he had learned. The words he had uttered no longer seemed appropriate. It was almost as if, by passing it down a generation, he had been trying to find a way to get rid of his own bad feelings about himself.

Some years later he started a new job and crashed his brand new company car only five days after it had been on the road. Fortunately, he had not hurt himself at all. Feeling incredibly embarrassed and upset, he went to apologize to his boss. What he said to him was: 'Well, I'm sure you didn't do it on purpose. No problem. We'll get it sorted out and back on the road for you as quickly as possible.'

His boss had shown to him that there was a different way of acting in a similar situation, one that did not make the other person feel even worse than they felt already. He recognized he needed to unlearn the old script and to find a new one – one that was his own.

Obviously, we can never change our past; but we can alter the influence it has on our lives so that we have more choices available to us. If you are already in a relationship and you are *both* prepared to do this work then you are really lucky, because it is through our relationships with our partners that we have the greatest opportunities for healing and growth, far greater than all the work we might ever undertake on our own.

The good child may have become the good adult – or the victim, or the rebel. But that's not who we truly are. That's the protective layer we have put on in order to survive, in order to cope with the demands placed upon us by our families, our workplaces, the needs of our children, our spouses and society.

So do you want merely to survive – or do you want to *thrive*? Are you ready to throw away your old script and write a new one?

Becoming aware of the influence of our past, turning around those old messages, and letting go of the residual feelings and emotions are all ways to ensure we *thrive* and create the relationships we deserve – relationships that will acknowledge and nourish us.

Today can be the beginning of a new life for each of us. We can choose joy right now. We can share love today. We can live in delight starting at this moment. It doesn't matter how miserable our past has been. Our present can be full of joy and our future can be full of happiness. It doesn't matter if we are eight or eighty; we can still make our lives wonderful. Life isn't over until your last heartbeat. Start today, then, to make your heart beat with joy, love and light.

Joseph J. Mazzella

3

Discovering Yourself Inside and Out

What lies behind us, and what lies before us are tiny matters, compared to what lies within.

Ralph Waldo Emerson, author (1803–82)

How well do you know yourself? How much do you really listen to that inner part of you that is not always quick to assert itself against a louder, more familiar, more critical voice repeating messages from the past, which so often feed our uncertainty or fear and hold us back from being our true selves?

Think about it. How often have you stopped yourself from saying what you really wanted to because that critical past voice is saying 'You must be polite to people', or stopped yourself from phoning up your dream date because you tell yourself 'They can have anyone they want, why should they be interested in me?'

Yet beneath that critical, discouraging voice there is a small, persistent voice that cries out from the very core of us to be heard: the voice that is saying such things as, 'There has to be more to life than this' or 'You can be so much more'.

We may hear this smaller voice sometimes, but the world so many of us inhabit is so fast-paced and so driven, that we are too busy 'doing' to listen to our 'being'. To keep ourselves going we drink alcohol and caffeine and eat fast foods, all of which contribute to the frenetic pace we've created in our lives and perpetuate a cycle that stops us from paying attention to *how* we are and *who* we are, that is, how we feel, our attitudes and approach to life, the positive or negative energy we give out.

When we focus too much on 'doing' and neglect our 'being' then we tune out from that inner voice. In fact, many of us may not even be sure if we have an inner voice or soul.

So what would it be like to wake up to who you truly are, to recognize what it is that you really want from life, to acknowledge your strengths and overcome the fears that may get in the way of achieving what you really want? This chapter is all about increasing your awareness of who you are, so that you will be in a better position to be your natural self and, being yourself, create the kind of relationships where you feel valued and can flourish.

By the end of the chapter we hope you will have:
- recognized your own strengths and vulnerabilities;
- come to appreciate why knowing yourself better will help you choose the right partner for you;
- identified ways of building up and maintaining your self-love;
- increased your awareness of your own feelings and begun to develop a vocabulary for expressing your emotions.

Who are you really?

As you found out in the last chapter, we tend to take on the values we grew up with. For example, if we were brought up in a family where hugging was a way of expressing affection, then as adults we will probably hug people we are fond of. From our childhood experiences and how we perceived them we create an identity for ourselves which we may believe without questioning is the truth about who we are.

Some of us lose sight of ourselves in a relationship because we're not altogether sure who we are and what we want and need. It's no wonder so many relationships fail, because when the inner self starts to wake up and say 'Hey, let me have a say too', it's often done in ways that seem angry and resentful. We may well blame everyone else for our circumstances. Sometimes we are left with a sense of emptiness or resignation, perhaps a sense that there probably is more to life but we've no way of finding out.

The clearer we become about who we are, the easier it is to recognize what is good for us and what the gifts are that we have to offer.

Jocasta's Story

Jocasta was the youngest child in her family. Her parents regarded her behaviour as much more challenging than that of her elder brother, who always toed the line. When dealing with Jocasta's behaviour, her parents often got angry and frustrated with her. However, later on they affectionately told other people stories about her antics, saying, for example, 'Jocasta was very naughty that day, but she's a really lively character'.

This resulted in Jocasta taking on board some mixed messages about herself. On the one hand, the way her parents dealt with her 'rebellious' behaviour resulted in the perception that she was a difficult child and caused grief and distress to her parents. On the other hand, from hearing her parents tell stories about her she learned that being a rebel was also a quality to be commended and held in affection.

In adulthood these messages influenced how Jocasta lived and behaved. She developed a drive and determination that supported her in achieving some major goals in her life, particularly her career. However, she was plagued by self-doubt and uncertainty because she had translated her parents' past criticism of her into a belief that she wasn't good enough, and in her adult life she secretly sought to be liked and approved of.

This meant that at times, rather than being demanding, she could be the complete opposite and let people walk all over her. As a result, she usually formed relationships with people who were attracted to her because she was strong; but as time went on, her partners did not relate so well to her self-doubt and vulnerability.

During coaching, Jocasta became aware of how her inability to accept her own vulnerable side was reflected in her choice of partners. Once she started to accept that this was part of who she was and that she was OK being that person, she began to form relationships with people who could accept all the aspects of her personality and identity, including both her strengths and her weaknesses.

When we ask people at our workshops 'Who are you really?' many people hesitate, take a deep breath and then have to think very hard before answering. In trying to answer this question, it can be helpful to take the first response that comes into your head and play with what it means. If you get stuck, try to think of a metaphor or symbol that represents who you are. When Mary was first asked this question, what immediately entered her head was 'I'm a Geordie lass'. When she thought around this statement she came up with many important qualities that resonated with her identity: Geordies are from the north-east of England – a cold, windswept part of the country where many people have suffered a degree of hardship, but where people are also renowned for their friendliness, festive spirit and the value they place on community. Mary could relate these characteristics to her own qualities of tenacity, always seeking to win out over adversity, earthiness, a sense of fun and a love of people.

Try this out for yourself in the following exercise.

EXERCISE: WHO ARE YOU REALLY?

Think of a statement or a metaphor – the first one you can come up with – that identifies you, and write it in your journal.

Now see if you can explore your answer further. To what extent does it represent who you really are? To what extent are you being that person now? Does the metaphor of you represent who you are really or how you want to be?

If you ask yourself this question at different times, you may find you come up with different answers. In Ariana's case, she came up with 'I'm half-Dutch, half-Czechoslovakian', 'I'm a doggy mum', 'I'm a divorcee', 'I'm a city seaside dweller', 'I'm a lover of life' and 'I'm childless'. All of these are relevant to Ariana's identity; there are, after all, many facets that make up each unique individual. For each such statement you make about yourself, explore what it really means to who you are as a person and what it tells you about how far the life you are living now allows you to be the real you.

In your journal, create a column entitled 'Who I Really Am' and list three or more identity statements that represent yourself. Alongside this column, create another column entitled 'Qualities That I Possess in Relation to My Identity'. Then list both the good and the bad qualities that you possess in relation to your individual identity statements. Be honest with yourself. This is all about accepting the whole of who you are.

Why do you want a relationship?

Many of us look for a relationship to help us feel better about ourselves, to fill in the gaps and to make us feel whole. Some people describe this as pieces of a jigsaw fitting together. However, if you're relying on someone else to help you feel all right then you are giving away your personal power and putting yourself in a very vulnerable and dependent position.

A model called the 'OK Corral', which was developed by psychologist Eric Berne, looks at the different life positions we take that represent how much we value ourselves and others (see diagram below). These positions colour our experiences and affect how we interact with others and the overall approach we take to our lives.

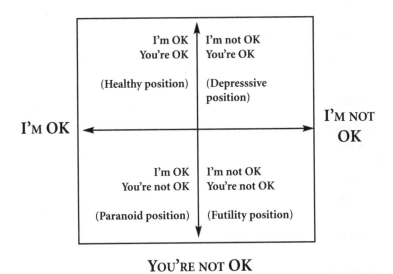

YOU'RE OK

I'm OK
You're OK

(Healthy position)

I'm not OK
You're OK

(Depresssive position)

I'M OK ⟵⟶ I'M NOT OK

I'm OK
You're not OK

(Paranoid position)

I'm not OK
You're not OK

(Futility position)

YOU'RE NOT OK

If your life position is *I'm OK with me, you're OK with me*, then you are likely to view yourself as lovable and good to be around. You will decide that other people are lovable and good to be around too and will see yourself and others as trustworthy.

If your position is *I'm not OK with me, you're OK with me*, you may well find yourself in positions where you are the loser and feeling as though you are the 'victim'.

A position of *I'm OK with me, you're not OK with me* may initially appear to be a winning formula because you will be out there getting what you want. However, when you hold this position, you are putting the other person down and people will eventually become discontented with this and reject you. Long-term relationships will prove hard to sustain.

Finally, if you take the position *I'm not OK with me, you're not OK with me*, then your world looks pretty dismal. You may perceive yourself as unlovable and others as incapable of supporting you. You will look at life as a combination of rejecting and being rejected.

The life position we take can be incredibly powerful in terms of how we see ourselves and others, and how we create what we want in our lives. Our positions can vary from one situation to another. Someone who has a hugely successful career because they take an 'I'm OK with me, you're OK with me' position in their work may have little success in relationships because they may hold an 'I'm not OK with me, you're OK with me' position when it comes to intimacy.

EXERCISE: WHAT'S YOUR LIFE POSITION?

Take another look at the four life positions in the table opposite; in your journal, note the following

- Which life position(s) do you relate to most?
- In what situations do you see yourself as totally OK, and in what others might you see either yourself or the other person as not OK?

Harry's and Debbie's stories provide some further examples of how these life positions can affect our relationships.

Harry's Story

Harry had not had a relationship for some time and had been quite depressed as a result. He met Julie, whom he regarded as extremely attractive and with whom he shared certain interests and values, including the desire to settle down and have a family. They had a whirlwind romance and all seemed perfect.

Harry was so besotted with Julie that he gave up on what he really wanted. He loved the bright lights of the city and enjoyed his metropolitan work and lifestyle. However, when they got married, to fit in with what Julie wanted and despite some reservations about the changes he was making, he agreed to move to a part of the country that was close to her family but where he knew no one, all because he wanted to 'keep her happy'.

He took a less satisfying but more financially rewarding job, to which he had to commute a long way, so that he could make the increased mortgage payments on the expensive house they had bought. They had two children, but he rarely got to see them because of the hours he was away at work, and he became increasingly exhausted and stressed.

When old friends challenged him on the apparent imbalance in the relationship, Harry acknowledged it but responded that he felt he had no choice as his love for Julie was all that mattered to him.

Eventually the relationship began to suffer. Communication between Julie and Harry was affected by his exhaustion, and Julie felt unhappy with bringing the children up virtually single-handed, even though Harry was doing his best to help out by looking after the kids when he was there. Despite all his efforts, the stresses and strains began to take their toll. The pair talked less and less and became more and more isolated from each other. Eventually Julie confessed that she had been seeing someone else and she ended the marriage.

Harry was devastated. He had devoted his entire existence to keeping Julie and the children happy and now that the marriage was over he felt he had nothing to show for it.

Harry had sacrificed himself and his needs and desires in his search for love. He entered the relationship under the misapprehension that if he did everything for Julie and kept her happy, all would be well. This fulfilled his need to be loved because he felt good about caring for someone else; he saw her needs as more important than his own and for the initial phase of their relationship this worked.

However, Harry could not sustain the position he got himself into. He suffered from the mounting pressures of taking responsibility for both Julie's and his own happiness and, in effect, ended up achieving the complete opposite to what he wanted. He entered the relationship from a position of being not OK about himself, and in trying to feel OK by caring for someone else he ended up perpetuating his original position.

If he'd come to the relationship from a place of wholeness, where he had felt OK about himself, whether he was in a relationship or not, he might have been far less willing to give up on himself. Perhaps he and Julie could have negotiated a way to meet both their needs, resulting in a very different outcome.

On the other hand, some people derive their strength and sense of self-love from creating a situation where, in order to feel OK about themselves, the other person has to feel not OK.

Debbie's Story

Debbie regarded herself as a real flirt. She flirted with life and attracted lots of men. Deep down, though, she lacked confidence in herself and needed attention from a wide variety of people to bolster her self-esteem.

She married young and enjoyed being in a long-term relationship. However, she continued to flirt her way through life and this caused problems in her marriage, as her husband disliked how she behaved with other men. Despite liking being married and loving her husband, she sometimes felt constrained by the relationship; she felt it cramped her style. She wasn't having as much fun and attention as she had when she was single, and she missed the boost it had given her self-esteem.

Indirectly, she took these negative feelings out on her husband, through digs and subtle put-downs. She would make belittling comments to him about how he looked or about his lack of performance in the bedroom and, over time, his confidence eroded. The better she felt about herself the less good he felt about himself, and that was the pattern in their relationship. After tolerating the situation for over ten years, Debbie's husband eventually realized the extent to which he was compromising himself and ended the marriage.

At the root of both Harry's and Debbie's situations was a need to feel good about themselves; though their strategies were very different, they both depended on other people to feel OK about themselves.

Feeling good about ourselves in our own right, not at the expense of someone else or at the cost of our own fulfilment, is important whether we are in a relationship or not. Therefore, we want to focus on how you can feel really good about yourself by increasing and affirming your sense of self-love and confidence, so that you don't have to rely on a relationship to make you believe that you are fundamentally OK. If you accept and love yourself, whether you are in a relationship or not, this will not only give you an increased sense of personal power and choice, but will also attract people to you who value themselves and will value you too.

Have you ever noticed that when you feel good, then good things seem to happen? And similarly, when we feel bad, we seem to get hit by further crisis? Well, the same goes for the people we attract. The more we work on looking after ourselves and building up our strengths and personal resources, then the more likely it is that we will attract and be attracted to people who will be in tune with what we want in our lives.

First love yourself

In the world of personal development there are many famous phrases. We believe that 'learning to love yourself' is at the root of everything. Time and time again, both in our own experiences and in those of our clients and friends, we see that what creates success in relationships, careers and life as a whole is a healthy self-regard and sense of self-love.

Let's be clear here about what we mean by success. It's easier to start by saying what we don't think it is. We don't think success is having a career at the cost of quality time, sleep, relaxation and leisure. We don't think it's having lots of money but really awful relationships. Nor do we think it's a relationship where one person does all the compromising.

Our definition of a successful life is one where there is balance, where individuals are able to love and accept themselves with all their strengths and flaws, and, through being themselves, to create relationships and opportunities that fulfil them and others around them. You may think this sounds a little idealistic, but the truth is that in learning to love and accept ourselves, we are also learning to accept and love others. It is not truly possible to have the one without the other.

Why must we love ourselves first?

If we don't genuinely love who we are, then what we do for other people often requires a payback, some way of meeting our need for love and appreciation. In an emergency on an aeroplane, if the oxygen masks appear, we are required to put our own mask on first before we can be of any help to others. This is not about being selfish; it's about recognizing that unless we look after our own needs we will not have sufficient resources to look after the needs of others.

Likewise, self-love is about respecting and honouring ourselves, so that others can do the same. If we show loving care and kindness to ourselves, then we are creating a model for others to treat us in the same way. If others don't show us this respect, then our self-respect will enable us to end a relationship that is not OK with us before it becomes damaging.

MARY'S STORY: I have a really fun, mischievous streak in me and when I was younger, less loving of myself and less confident, I often turned that humour against myself and encouraged others to laugh at me too. As I've matured, my sense of self-love is much greater; I still possess the same cheeky humour, but I don't turn it on myself, nor do I turn it on others. I use it to create fun in my life and to turn to the good situations that otherwise might be challenging for me or others.

So what stops us from loving ourselves?

It's easy to talk about the importance of loving and respecting ourselves, but it's not so easy at times to feel or act that way. The picture we build of ourselves goes a long way back into our past. Some of the work we've been doing in the previous chapters looks at the messages we may have taken on board when we were very young and how these might impact on how we act now.

When it comes to self-love we are dealing with deeply embedded messages about what is good or bad about us, what is right or wrong, which we have turned into our own truth about ourselves. We have then developed ways to survive despite these messages, and these survival strategies shape the pattern of our strengths and weaknesses.

Jackie's Story

Jackie learned as a child that it was easier for her to give up on her needs in order to help others. As an adult she developed great skills in helping other people. On the one hand, this was a strength, particularly in her chosen profession as a group counsellor; on the other, she was so attuned to supporting others that getting her own needs met, particularly in an intimate relationship, was a real challenge for her.

So, although she appeared sympathetic and understanding to her partners, underneath she was quietly fuming because she was tired of bending over backwards for other people. As a result, she often sabotaged her relationships, either withdrawing from them emotionally as an indirect way to punish her partner, or, occasionally, by exploding in a furious and irrational rage.

Getting her needs met in 'healthy' ways (i.e. coming from a position of 'I'm OK with me and you're OK with me') is something she is working on in her coaching.

Our levels of self-love rise and fall. If you look back on your adult life, irrespective of what happened when you were younger, there will be times in your life when you felt better about yourself than others.

There are 'healthy' things you can introduce into your life that will improve your sense of well-being and encourage a greater sense of self-love, and that's what the rest of this chapter is about. What is important is that you come from a place of honesty about yourself: completing the rest of the exercises in this chapter would be pretty futile if you did not approach them candidly.

Know your strengths

Our deepest fear is not that we are inadequate.
Our deepest fear is that we are powerful beyond measure.
It is our light, not our darkness that frightens us.
We ask ourselves, who am I to be brilliant, gorgeous, talented, fabulous?
Actually, who are you not to be?
You are a child of God. Your playing small doesn't serve the world.
There's nothing enlightening about shrinking so that other people won't feel insecure around you.
We are all meant to shine, as children do.
We were born to make manifest the glory of God that is within us. Its not just in some of us, it's in everyone.
And as we let our own light shine, we unconsciously give other people permission to do the same.
As we are liberated from our fear, our presence automatically liberates others.
From *A Return to Love* by Marianne Williamson (b.1952)

If we want other people to see how great we are, then we have to start acknowledging our strengths and qualities to ourselves first. Yet, as Marianne Williamson suggests, we are often more frightened of our greatness than of our weaknesses, and that is why we so often sabotage ourselves, so we don't have to take the risk of being the great individual we really are. We play it safe.

We all probably know someone who has withdrawn from the whole notion of having a relationship because in the past they have been hurt too many times. They therefore avoid meeting people or, if someone is attracted to them, they very skilfully do something to turn that person away because it feels far too risky to get involved again.

The following pages contain a selection of exercises that provide you with the opportunity to look at your strengths. Some of you may feel uncomfortable doing these, but try to view this discomfort as a sign of growth and a shift towards doing things in a way that will serve you better than the ways in which you have done things in the past. By definition, stepping out of your comfort zone will feel strange, and you may feel fearful, but remember – the people who act with courage are those who take their fear with them.

Once you start to recognize and acknowledge what you bring to the world, then you will start to open up greater possibilities for yourself. In an approach known as 'Appreciative Inquiry', which was developed by researcher David Cooperrider, it has been shown that we grow in the direction in which we persistently ask questions. By looking at what has worked in the past, we can create a desirable future.

If you find these exercises difficult to tackle, we suggest you begin by selecting the one that is easiest for you to get started on and go from there. We strongly recommend you do as many of them as possible. We are all very skilful at giving ourselves a hard time, and often the way we view ourselves is completely different both from the way others see us and from the way we want to be living our lives.

It can be helpful to ask a friend to go through these exercises with you – someone who knows you and knows when you are not being honest with yourself.

EXERCISE: STRENGTHS INVENTORY

In your journal, note down as many things that you recognize as positive qualities about yourself or skills you possess. It doesn't matter what these are, or how big or small they are. What is important is that you recognize your own worth and note it down. For example, you may be good at listening to others or at parking a car in the smallest of spaces. Whatever you do well, note it down and acknowledge yourself for it.

List as many as you can and aim to add to your list every day for at least the next two weeks. This way you will notice your strengths on a daily basis.

EXERCISE: ASK FOR FEEDBACK

Send the following questions to as many friends as possible and ask them to write down their answers and send them to you. If you're uncomfortable about doing this, tell them why you are doing it; they are friends, after all, and most of the time people are pleased to be able to tell you what they like about you.

First, do the exercise yourself, imagining that you are your own friend. Then, compare what you said with what others say about you. How is that different?

- What do you see as my unique qualities?
- What is it you most value in me?
- If I were not in your life, what would you most miss about me?

EXERCISE: WHAT MAGAZINE ARE YOU?

This is a fun one! Imagine you are a magazine:

- What sort of magazine would you be?
- What sort of articles would appear?
- What market would you appeal to?

Ask others to tell you what sort of magazine they would describe you as.

EXERCISE: TURNING YOUR INTERNAL CRITIC INTO AN INTERNAL COACH

Our beliefs are transmitted to us through our thoughts, which we often express internally to ourselves as a critical voice. This voice can be very judgmental and dismissive, preventing us from taking risks, reinforcing perceived weaknesses and generally limiting us. While on the one hand it's important that we have a sense of security within ourselves, it's not so good that we achieve this through self-deprecation.

A more effective way to maintain a sense of internal security is to be less self-critical and more supportive of ourselves.

OBSERVING AS OPPOSED TO JUDGING

Try simply noticing your experiences, as opposed to criticizing yourself, and see how this affects your feelings. For example, let's say you run into someone to whom you are attracted and you go red and lose the ability to string two words together. Rather than saying to yourself, 'I am so stupid. How can I expect them to like me when I can't even speak in their company!', simply observe to yourself, 'When I meet X, I feel shy and lose my words.' And then think to yourself, 'How would I like to be when I see that person?' In asking yourself that question you are starting to open up possibilities for yourself.

Keep a record over the coming week of experiences in which you've let go of judging yourself and simply observed your experience instead.

- How does simply noticing impact on your feelings?
- How does this then impact on your behaviour?
- How does it impact on other people's behaviour?
- What difference does this make for you?
- What new possibilities are you creating for how things could be different for you?

You might also like to try doing this with your experiences of others. You know how easy it is to jump to the wrong conclusions about people. This then affects your overall picture of them and, as a result, you may then act negatively towards them. Well, see what happens if you stop judging them and simply observe what's going on instead, as though you were in a helicopter, looking down from way up high. And just notice what a difference that makes for you.

BE CURIOUS

As well as observing yourself and others, become inquisitive about your observations. Become your own coach as you ask yourself questions. It's by being curious and becoming more consciously aware of how we behave that we can start to look at whether it is working for us. For example, after noticing that you feel shy and become tongue-tied on meeting someone you like, ask yourself:

- Why do I do that?
- Is it an indication of how much I like them?
- How would I ideally like to act in this situation?
- What can I do to feel more confident around them?

Using questions beginning with 'what', 'where', 'when', 'why' and 'how' can help you to delve a bit further and will give you some insights that can be invaluable when it comes to making decisions about how you might prefer to act.

John's Story

John used to judge the raised pitch of his partner's voice as a whinge; he said it drove him nuts and this resulted in some serious arguments. In an attempt to improve their communication and avoid these arguments, when his partner used that tone of voice John literally stepped back and noted to himself his observations of his partner's behaviour and how that made him feel. This in itself gave him enough room to make a choice about how he might respond, and he found he was far less likely to react badly having given himself the space to observe in this way.

EXERCISE: DEVELOP YOUR OWN POSITIVE AFFIRMATIONS

An affirmation is a declaration. It's a statement designed to instil a commitment and message.

When we first came across 'affirmations' we were quite dismissive: they appeared false and unreal to us. However, we now both recognize that having one, two or three pertinent and really positive affirmations can be empowering, particularly when we are faced with a challenging situation.

A well-chosen affirmation is:

- a very useful reminder of who we really are;
- a positive message we can repeat to ourselves regularly;
- a support in loving ourselves, in contrast to the critical messages we may be carrying from our past.

To be effective, a positive affirmation should:

- be short and easy to remember or keep to hand (e.g. short enough to have on the opening page of your mobile phone);
- be stated in the present tense;
- be pertinent to you, so that when you say it to yourself it touches you;
- inspire and empower you;
- create a high sense of self-love for yourself.

Here is a selection that we've come across. You may want to play around with these and to add more of your own. Read through each one and identify the three that are most valuable for you.

I am loving.	I am lovable.	I love myself.
I am powerful.	I am worthy.	I am sensitive.
I respect myself.	I am special.	I am OK as I am.
I trust myself.	I am strong.	I am beautiful.
I am inspiring.	I am peaceful.	I am brilliant.
I am daring.	I am great.	I am enough.
I am me.	I am sexy.	I am strong.
I am worthy.	I am capable.	I am good enough.

Louise's Story

Louise had recently started seeing someone who teased her in a way that was derogatory and undermining . She wanted to ask him not to do this, but felt vulnerable because she really liked her new boyfriend. In the past she would have probably put up with being teased, but she kept reminding herself through her affirmations that she was 'a worthy woman' and when she phoned her boyfriend to tell him how she felt, she had her three most potent affirmations on cards in front of her by the phone – 'I am worthy', 'I am powerful' and 'I respect myself'.

This spurred her on and gave her a sense of her own strength. Her boyfriend's response to her request was to laugh and tease her again. Although it was hard for her, Louise knew in her heart of hearts that she did not want to get involved with someone who would not respect her, so she chose to end the relationship then and there. She said that having the affirmations written in front of her helped her keep her resolve, and she is now proud that she managed to look after herself and was able to stay with what was important to her.

EXERCISE: CREATE A SUPPORT NETWORK

Being around people who give us a hard time does not enhance our confidence or sense of self. So, start being more discerning and surround yourself with people with whom you feel good. This is not about being selfish or mean, as some people might try and tell you.

It's important to look after ourselves and, once again, as our own coaches, we need to check in with ourselves from time to time as to how we feel when we are with certain people. This does not mean surrounding yourself with a collection of sycophants, but seeking out people who genuinely offer you loving friendship, who value you for who you are, warts and all. Compassionately sharing your needs and requirements with another can really open up your relationship to greater things.

If you have to be around people who might criticize or judge you or drain your energy, then go for damage limitation and either meet them on neutral territory or set limits on the time you spend with them. Tell them the impact their behaviour is having on you and what it is you want for the relationship in the future.

Mark's Story

There was no doubt that Mark loved his mother and that she wanted the best for him. However, he found her constant questioning and suggestions about how he should run his life exhausting. Mark heard his mother's words not as loving but as nagging. So, to counteract this he acknowledged his appreciation of her love for him and the interest she had in his life, but asked that whenever they met or spoke on the phone they kept their discussion of what he was doing to a maximum of ten minutes.

His mother was at first taken aback but agreed. As a result they now have a closer relationship and are able to have conversations about all sorts of things that never got a look-in before.

Own up to your weaknesses

The more we seek perfection, the more it will elude us.

Anon.

While it's really important to stay in touch with our strengths, it is also important to acknowledge that we have weaknesses too. This is not so you can start beating yourself up about them, but because you can genuinely love yourself only when you recognize and accept those parts of yourself that are not so perfect.

Often, our strengths and weaknesses are very closely aligned. Earlier on in this chapter, we saw how Jackie was so good at helping other people to meet their needs that she found it hard to ask for her own to be fulfilled. Strengths that are overdeveloped can become weaknesses.

If we can be really honest with ourselves about our negative aspects we will find it easier to embrace them (they are a part of us, after all). Then, having properly acknowledged them, we are in a position to choose ways to counteract any negative impact they might have.

Rob's Story

Rob was enormously organized and capable, both at work and at home, and proud of it. No problem was insurmountable as far as he was concerned. He prided himself on being a 'Mr Fix-It', and loved it when people came to him for help and he was able to give them the advice they sought. The trouble was, however, he often doled out advice when it wasn't asked for, and felt frustrated when people didn't seem to want him to solve their problems.

His wife, Christine, lacked the confidence that he had and over the years had come to rely on him totally. He would not only sort out their finances, but would also book the holidays, organize the school run, cook for dinner parties, even return books to the library. She had wanted to do these things, but had learned over the years that whatever she did, Rob's way was better (or at least he said it was), and so she had just given up trying to assert herself.

Following a couple of life-changing personal empowerment workshops that she attended, Christine felt it was time to take back control of her life. She proposed to Rob that they seek counselling together to renegotiate how their marriage could work. He refused because he was 'not prepared to let anyone else tell me how to run my life'.

Five years on, she is now a busy office manager for a local insurance firm, living on her own (except when the children are back from university) and regularly seeing a boyfriend who adores her. She is loving her new-found independence. Rob is still organized, but feels isolated and alone. There is no doubt he is a man with great strengths, but his inability to be vulnerable and accept that he might not be perfect cost him his marriage.

EXERCISE: STRENGTHS AND WEAKNESSES

In your journal, note your answers to the following questions:

- In reviewing your strengths, which ones do you recognize that you overdo so they start to hinder you and become weaknesses?
- What about other weaknesses? What do you know to be true about you that is less than perfect?
- To what degree have you accepted that this is part of who you are?
- What action might you want to take to counteract the impact a particular weakness may have?

Your feelings

> *It is the place of feeling that binds us or frees us.*
>
> Jack Kornfield

We all have feelings, and yet some of us have a hard time admitting to them, let alone giving expression to them. How many of us remember, as children, being told, 'Oh, you shouldn't feel that way' when we expressed, say, annoyance over something. You may even have been punished for expressing your true feelings about something.

Many of us have pushed our feelings underground, because to express them can just seem too risky. We may fear failure, ridicule and rejection, so we bottle our feelings up or file them away.

We have seen how our thoughts can change our beliefs and attitudes; another key part of being authentic is to acknowledge our truest underlying feelings.

If we are feeling anxious or hurt about something, it is important to acknowledge that in ourselves. If we don't acknowledge our feelings or allow them to emerge then we are denying their existence. But they don't go away. Unexpressed feelings can wreak havoc on our health – it takes more energy to keep a feeling down than it does to allow it to rise to the surface and express it – and we may find ourselves suffering from stress and even nervous exhaustion.

Allowing ourselves to feel our feelings, and learning to articulate them, enables us to relate fully and openly to the outside world and to the people with whom we want to have relationships.

How often do you say something is fine when you know it's not? Many of us, acting out the role of 'good child' when we were growing up, bottled up our feelings and still find it hard to give voice to them now. Often we fear that we are not really nice people, so that if we express all of ourselves we will get found out for who we really are. Most of us don't want to be disliked, and so it's no wonder many of us try to be someone the world will like and end up pretending to be someone we're not.

But if we do this to the detriment of how we feel, then we may pay a heavy price. Being able to recognize and name our feelings is an important part of being in any relationship, because unacknowledged feelings have a strange way of making themselves heard in a way that may be extremely uncomfortable and sometimes harmful.

When we don't recognize our feelings of anxiety or repressed annoyance, these feelings build up over time until they either explode in huge outbursts of anger or, turned inwards, result in depression – sometimes described, indeed, as 'anger turned inwards'. If you have not learned how to express your feelings and therefore never had those feelings acknowledged by your partner you are probably taking on the role of 'good child' in the relationship, which can give rise to underlying discontent and ultimately relationship breakdown.

The painted smile

We all know the image of the clown who wears the mask with a painted smile but underneath is a sad person, afraid to reveal who they really are to the world because they just don't feel OK enough in themselves to do so.

What we're talking about here is about the ability to be *authentic*. Being authentic means being clear about our feelings as well as our beliefs and values: telling the truth about everything that makes us who we are. Being authentic means taking responsibility for who we are and not losing ourselves (or bits of ourselves) when we are in relationships with other people.

Ask yourself:

- Does the way you reveal yourself on the outside match up to who you are on the inside?
- If not, in what way does it not?

Many comedians use their humour as a mask or shield to deflect attention away from themselves. This stops others from getting too close; it repels intimacy. There are many well-known examples of famous comics who suffered recurrent bouts of depression. No wonder. It must be a huge struggle to live up to a hilarious extrovert image when the person inside is somebody completely different.

Think of a time when you felt hurt by a remark someone had made to you but chose to laugh to cover up the way you were truly feeling. Maybe you do this a lot, maybe hardly ever; but, even if you've only done it once, you will recognize what we are talking about here.

Think about yourself and your intimate relationships. How much do you try to please your partner at the expense of what is really true for you? How much of you do you conceal in the process?

In the early stages of a relationship, how much of who you truly are do you feel safe to reveal? At what point do you let the mask drop... if ever?

EXERCISE: WHAT MASKS DO YOU WEAR?

Which of the following masks do you wear? Tick as many as you recognize.

	Yes	No
Mr Macho	☐	☐
Ms Agreeable	☐	☐
Mr Attentive	☐	☐
Ms Ever-So-Interested	☐	☐
Ms Immaculate	☐	☐
Mr I'm-So-Interesting	☐	☐
Ms I-So-Enjoy-Cooking	☐	☐
Mr I'm-So-Amusing	☐	☐
Mr Cool	☐	☐
Ms Sorted	☐	☐

- What is it that you are concealing behind the masks that you fear revealing about you?
- Some people never reveal all of themselves to anyone. Is that you?
- How much are you prepared to show your true self and under what circumstances?
- Where does your mask come from?

We wear these masks as defences against what we perceive to be a hostile world, to help us survive, to keep us feeling safe, because we are:

- afraid to rock the boat;
- trying to be who (we think) our partner wants us to be;
- trying to hide our imperfections;
- trying to agree;
- trying not to be a burden.

But this feeling of safety is an illusion. If we are struggling to be what someone else wants us to be, the mask may well crack, and that can cost us many things, including our health.

- What is it costing you to hide behind your mask and keep you from being authentic?
- What is it costing you to keep the mask in place?

Describing feelings

We aren't all taught to express our feelings and many of us don't possess a vocabulary with which to describe our emotions. Yet language is often the way we make sense of our experience, and so it is really helpful to build up a vocabulary of words that express the varying degrees of our emotions.

EXERCISE: BUILDING A VOCABULARY FOR YOUR FEELINGS

Our feelings tend to fall into five main areas:

ANGER   SADNESS   FEAR   HAPPINESS   LOVE

What descriptive words do you use to describe each of these? In your journal note the words you associate with each. For example, for ANGER you might choose 'irritated' or 'furious', for SAD you could be 'deflated' or 'melancholic', for FRIGHTENED you could use 'excited' or 'terrified', you could replace HAPPY with 'content' or 'ecstatic', or for LOVING you could choose 'tender' or 'adoring'.

Below is a list of words to help you that might relate to some of your feelings, but please only refer to this if you are stuck. It is far better if you can come up with your own:

calm	depressed	competent	inadequate	sad
anxious	determined	annoyed	excited	happy
disgusted	joyful	inspired	hopeless	passionate
powerful	afraid	relaxed	indifferent	ashamed
embarrassed	relieved	fearful	tempted	stressed
insecure	hopeful	loving	uneasy	competitive

timid	trapped	confident	brave	distrustful
lonely	ecstatic	frustrated	irritated	inspired
overwhelmed	victorious	angry	withdrawn	ambivalent
disappointed	nervous	worthy	sympathetic	despairing
childlike	comfortable	bored	affectionate	vulnerable
envious	helpless	grateful	tense	distant
needy	optimistic	repulsed	upset	guilty
content	discouraged	lustful	furious	deflated

Taking responsibility for your feelings

Now look at the following list of words. How do these differ from those in the list included in the exercise above?

rejected	humiliated	cheated	loved	alienated
adored	controlled	hurt	criticized	let down
ignored	manipulated	cherished	neglected	mistreated

In grammatical terms, they are all the past participles of transitive verbs: that is, they describe things that other people have *done* to us.

These are the words we use in the stories we make up in our heads about how others are treating us.

However, they are not *feelings* but *thoughts*: they are our own interpretation of what others may have done to us. Indirectly, we are putting the responsibility or blame on to someone else for how we feel. We are, in fact, making an assumption that the other person is rejecting, cheating, loving or cherishing us.

We often think we are the only ones who feel the way we do; but we all have feelings, and at one time or another we will all have felt angry, frightened or sad, just as we will also have felt happy and loving. What it is crucial to realize is that our feelings are precisely *our* feelings, and if we blame other people for 'making us' feel what we feel, we are giving away our power and closing down choices for ourselves.

If someone speaks to you in a way that you perceive as patronizing and you feel humiliated, you are placing your own interpretation on how they spoke to you and your reaction is likely to be a reflection of your own feelings of vulnerability. If you had been feeling good about yourself, you might not have let the way they spoke to you bother you at all. It's *your* reaction and it comes from you, no one else; we can't expect other people to be responsible for how we feel.

If you object that you can't choose how you feel, then this would suggest that your feelings are very strong and that you're allowing them to take over. As in most things, it's important to strike a balance. On the one hand, being in touch with our feelings means we can let them guide us in our decisions and actions. On the other hand, if we llow our feelings to overtake us, we either lose the power to express ourselves or find we can only express them in unhelpful ways – for example, bursting into tears when we've reached the end of our tether as a result of not acknowledging our feelings before. When our emotions overwhelm us they inhibit our ability to talk about them. Understanding our feelings can help us find that balance.

Notice the difference between these two statements:
- 'She has hurt me so badly. I'll never get over it.'
- 'I feel really sad that our relationship has come to an end. But although I know it will take time for the pain to heal, I will come through it.'

Which is the victim statement? Which is the more powerful of the two?

There is a difference between seeing yourself as a *victim* of circumstances, and therefore powerless to change anything, and owning your true feelings and knowing that it is within your power to do something about your situation.

But before we can do anything about our feelings, we need to recognize them as they arise, rather than let them continue to hide behind the mask and pretend to ourselves that things are different from how they actually are.

Where and how do you feel your feelings?

When we have an emotional response, more often than not we have a physiological reaction too. Think about it: does your face flush if you are embarrassed? If you are waiting to make a speech to a large group, do you get butterflies in your stomach? This is all perfectly normal.

Part of building up our awareness of our feelings is to start noticing where in our bodies we have a reaction, what the sensation is like and which emotion we can relate this sensation to. Try to stay aware of your body and what you are feeling physically as it really can serve you in recognizing, managing and expressing your emotions

EXERCISE: EMOTIONS IN THE BODY

The purpose of this exercise is to allow you to get in touch with how you feel your feelings in your body. Follow the step-by-step instructions carefully and note your observations in your journal.

- Sit comfortably in a chair with both your feet on the floor and your arms loosely by your sides.
- Select one emotion to focus on.
- Close your eyes and remember a time when you felt this emotion: e.g., for 'anger' a time when you lost your temper.
- Take between 30 and 60 seconds at the most to get in touch with the feeling you felt at the time.
- Now see what sensation there is in your body.
- Whereabouts in your body are you feeling this?
- What is the sensation like?
- Is it moving or still?
- Is it hard or soft, smooth, rough, or sharp?
- Come back to the present, open your eyes and note down in your journal the sensations you felt.

Repeat this exercise for other emotions and see how your physiological reaction varies.

Logging your emotions

Some people may find this exercise difficult; if we're very used to not feeling, it may be hard to detect any bodily sensations at all. A way to start building up your awareness is to log your emotions.

EXERCISE: EMOTIONS LOG

Select an ordinary day and commit yourself to stop on the hour (or every two hours) and notice what your mood is like and how you are feeling physically at that moment. It's really important that you tune in and get in touch with how you feel now: not how you felt five minutes ago or half an hour ago. Every time you stop, write your observations down in your journal. At the end of the day, review what you have written.

	Day 1	Day 2	Day 3	Day 4	Day 5
Morning					
Midday					
Afternoon					
Evening					

- What can you notice?
- How much do your emotions change from one hour to the next, or from moment to moment?

To keep improving your sensitivity to your emotions you might want to repeat this exercise regularly, perhaps once a month.

Alternatively, you could monitor your emotions over a whole week. That way you could start to discern whether there are any patterns, such as only feeling ecstatic in the morning!

Notice again that some of the feelings you initially identify, like *rejected* and *criticized*, might put the blame on others and so get in the way of your owning your true feelings. Other responses, such as *repulsed* or *irritated*, are also likely to be masking your true feelings. You may need to explore further and ask yourself:

- What's the feeling behind that feeling?
- And what's the feeling behind that?

Keep on asking yourself the question until you get to the root of what it is you are avoiding feeling – and then notice the stories you tell yourself that prevent you from really getting in touch with your true feelings.

Patrick's Story

Patrick came to coaching because he was lonely and hadn't ever really had a long-standing close relationship. The first couple of months of coaching were hard. He was resistant to taking responsibility for doing any work and expected his coach to provide him with all the answers. He wanted a relationship and could not understand why he needed to look to himself first of all.

His coach confronted him with the choices he had. He wanted a relationship, but how much was he prepared to give of himself in order to get one? Did his lack of participation in the coaching reflect a similar attitude towards finding a partner and involving himself in a relationship? Patrick said he wanted a relationship badly and his coach's feedback helped his self-awareness.

For the first time he shared how frightened he was. He had had some really bad experiences in the past, for example he had been bullied at school, where no one had liked him. His way to deal with this had been to remain aloof, strait-laced and rather critical in his manner. Admitting this fear was a breakthrough in beginning to understand and express his feelings more openly. Patrick realized that life could be much richer if he shared his feelings with others. As he started to do this, he began to build warmer and deeper relationships. He continued with his coaching and also attended some personal development programmes that helped him get in touch with expressing his other emotions.

Although we have looked at five main areas of emotions in terms of how we express ourselves, at the end of the day, according to *A Course in Miracles* by the Foundation for Inner Peace, there are only two fundamental emotions that humans experience – *love* and *fear*. For example, anger is often a way of masking fear, which we may be ashamed of feeling.

So, think about these questions:
- How do you feel and how do you behave when you are fearful?
- How do you feel and how do you behave when you are loving?

Once you get to this point and can really own your feelings, you can begin to control them rather than be controlled by them; you can then shine the spotlight on your feelings and choose how you want to deal with them. You might want to use the exercise on on pages 34–6 to deal with some of them.

Towards authenticity

By building up your self-awareness, getting a clearer sense of your identity, recognizing and accepting your strengths and weaknesses, and getting in touch with your true feelings you are getting closer to learning to love yourself and others in a truly real and honest way that resonates from the very core of you. This is what is known as authenticity; and the more you are authentic in yourself, the more you will find it easier to make loving choices that work for you, not only in relationships but also in other areas of your life.

4

Love Your Own Life First

*There's this question that gets asked on the show,
'Who is Samantha going to end up with?' and I
think it's not about ending up with someone.
This is your life, it's not your life with Sam or
George – that's part of it – but it's your life.*

Kim Cattrall (b.1956), *Sex and the City* actress

This chapter is all about making sure you create a great life for yourself, a life that supports the real you, which you enjoy and in which you can flourish. Sure, having a fulfilling relationship is part of that; but it is not all of your life, and putting all your eggs in the relationship basket in pursuit of happiness is like investing all your savings in one stock – nothing is guaranteed and there is a high risk of being left destitute.

Whether or not you are in a relationship right now, one thing that is really important for relationship success is to make sure that every area of your life is working for you and fulfils you. The good life is one that is balanced and integrated – so that different areas support one other and fit together easily – healthy and fun; a life that energizes us and enables us to be our best in all areas.

This might sound idealistic, but it is possible. Of course, things will not always be perfect; but if we aim to create a life along these lines, then even when we face bumps along the way, they are so much easier to handle. Even if you are in a relationship, you owe it to yourself to let this relationship be a part of your complete life rather than the reason your life is complete. Live a really great life and it will enrich your relationship, rather than your relationship being the only richness in your life. The same is true if you are not in a relationship.

Remember Harry's story on page 54? He sold out on himself and did everything for his partner only to be totally compromised when all his efforts still could not make her happy and she ended the relationship.

Ask yourself:
- to what extent are you putting all the focus on finding a relationship in order to have what you perceive as a complete life;
  or:
- how much are you selling out on yourself, your own well-being, the things that make you happy, in order to keep your relationship going.

We would like to encourage you to focus on creating a great life for yourself, with or without a partner, so that you are in a much more discerning position when it comes to meeting a partner or making decisions as part of a relationship. Not only does this increase the likelihood of your being happy in your relationship; it also adds to your overall ability to attract more of what you really want into your life. If you're feeling great, doing things you love and living life in tune with your needs and values, then you are going to have much more positive energy to attract the sort of partner you want.

So, by the time you finish this chapter we hope you will have:
- reviewed how your life is as a whole;
- recognized what you need in order to feel and be your best;
- begun to look at and deal with some of the things you are tolerating about your life;
- appreciated how you can influence your own levels of attraction;
- learned how to live a fulfilling life, with or without a partner;
- developed an action plan for making the most of each area of your life.

Create a life you can honestly say you love!

You want more love in your life? Then start creating a life that you love.

Easy to say, not so easy to do? Well you'd be surprised how doing some really simple things can make a big difference to your overall sense of well-being and enjoyment of your life.

When you think about your ideal partner, how much are you the type of person *you* think *they* would be attracted to?

EXERCISE: LOOK AT YOUR LIFE BALANCE

This exercise takes you through some questions that will help you to assess how balanced your life is. Note your answers in your journal.

WHAT DO YOU DO FOR FUN, AND DO THESE THINGS GIVE YOU NATURAL ENERGY?

When we talk about 'natural energy' we mean energy that is not stimulated by caffeine, alcohol or drugs. These may well pep you up, but their influence is short-term and, ultimately, they have a depressing and draining effect on your health. So:

- What outlets do you have for doing things that you really enjoy, that you can lose yourself in, but not at a cost to your health?
- What interesting things can you talk about and share with others?

HOW MEANINGFUL AND FULFILLING DO YOU FIND YOUR WORK?

- Do you live to work or work to live?
- How passionate are you about what you do?
- Are your talents being used in your job?
- How often does work energize you and how often does it drain you?
- If you've had several jobs that have turned out the same way, might it be more to do with your own lack of fulfilment than the job?
- What would you rather do that would be an expression of your authentic self?

DO YOU HAVE A STRONG SUPPORT NETWORK OF FRIENDS AND COLLEAGUES?

As the poet John Donne famously said, 'No man is an island', and having a really strong network of people we can rely on to support us can make all the difference in turning adversity into triumph.

- If you don't have one already, what group of like-minded people could you draw together to share your hopes and dreams and to support one another in action?

HOW LOVING ARE YOUR RELATIONSHIPS?

- Whether you're in a romantic relationship or not, how loving are your other relationships?
- With whom, among your family members or friends, are you still holding on to old scores? Whom do you blame for past wrongs done to you?
- Which of your friends or family tell you they love you regularly? How often do you show or tell them you love them?

HOW WELL ARE YOUR FINANCES SORTED OUT?

It's very hard to be our true and best self if we are worried about debts or how to pay the bills. Similarly, seeking a partner in the hope that they will rescue us from our financial doldrums is not a powerful or stable base upon which to build a relationship. In turn, this might well influence us and cause us to compromise on other more important aspects of our life. Having a strong financial base has a direct influence on our overall sense of well-being.

- How stable are you financially?
- Can you provide for yourself financially or do you rely on others?
- Do you have enough savings to allow you to live for six months?
- Are all your assets adequately insured?
- Do you have a plan that will lead you into financial independence?

HOW ARE YOUR PHYSICAL HEALTH AND SELF-IMAGE?

Do you like what you see when you look in the mirror? Do you spend a lot of your time trying to make yourself look good and worrying about how you look with your clothes on or off? It's important to be your authentic self and make the most of who you are, whatever your shape, size, age or colour.

- How do you take care of yourself physically? Are you physically fit, do you eat a healthy diet?
- Do you wear clothes that make the most of yourself and that represent your personality?

DO YOU LIVE IN AN ENVIRONMENT THAT YOU LOVE AND THAT INSPIRES YOU?

- When you wake up in the morning are you pleased with your surroundings or do you feel depressed or irritated?
- What can you do to make where you live a more pleasant place?
- Is your space tidy or is everything hidden under pile of clutter?

WHAT DO YOU DO TO SUPPORT YOUR OWN GROWTH AND DEVELOPMENT?

- To what degree are you wanting to taking action, to learn and grow from your experiences?
- Are you open to accepting and rising to the challenges that you face in your life?
- How happy are you with yourself?

This chapter offers you an opportunity to take stock of your life as a whole and review your overall level of satisfaction in every area, not just your relationships. The 'Life Balance Spectrum' shown in the diagram on the opposite page divides your life into eight different

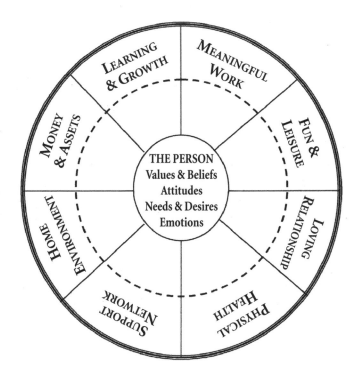

sections. The inner circle in the middle represents the core of you: your true self, your beliefs, values, emotions and needs. The surrounding sections represent each area of your life.

Thinking about who you are and how you want to live your life in tune with your true self, consider how satisfied you are with each area of your life. With a pencil, shade in each section of the spectrum to represent your level of satisfaction with that area of your life, starting from the inner circle and working your way out to the outside edge. The closer your shading is to the outside edge, the greater your level of satisfaction. If you're at the dotted line, you're halfway there.

EXERCISE: REVIEWING THE LIFE BALANCE SPECTRUM

The higher your level of satisfaction in each area of your life and the more even it is across the whole spectrum, the greater the levels of natural positive energy you'll possess. Review your overall life balance and level of satisfaction with each area of your life.

- Which areas of your life are you most happy with?
- Which areas of your life are you least happy with?
- What are the first three small steps that you could take that would contribute to your goal of living a life that you love?
- Are there areas in your life that appear to be more challenging or difficult for you to change than others?
- If so, where or from whom could you get help and support in order to take some positive action in these areas?
- Which area that needs to change would make the biggest difference now?

Now take a look at your diary. How many things do you have booked into it over the coming month that will really uplift you and make you feel great? What would it be like to try something completely different from your normal activities? Something that you have always wanted to do but never got round to? If you don't have at least one fun/ fulfilling activity booked in per week, then get going and book some in.

We've put together a list of potential activities and we're sure you can think of some of your own too.

- Meet up with friends.
- Take up singing.
- Go to a football match.
- Go to a concert.
- Take up ice-skating.
- Join a drama group.
- Learn to meditate.
- Take a walk in the country.
- Join a book club.

- Do an outdoor pursuit, e.g. walking, horse-riding, sailing.
- Have a picnic with friends.
- Visit a country pub.
- Visit a gallery.
- Take up yoga.
- Have a massage.
- Take up salsa dancing.
- Do a cookery class.

- Have a potluck supper: ask everyone to bring a dish and a friend.
- Do an exercise class.
- Take a trip to the theatre.
- Go to an art exhibition.
- Join a gym or learn a sport.
- Have a romantic night in with your partner.

So you've booked in some planned activities; what about spontaneity? What simple things can you do quite spontaneously on a daily basis that will help you and others around you feel better?

Below are some things that we do regularly – we wouldn't ask you to do anything we haven't tried ourselves! So although you might feel reluctant to try some of these, leave your inhibitions behind and go for it – you might even find you enjoy yourself!

- Pick up the phone to a long-lost friend or relative.
- Give some flowers to a stranger.
- Strike up a conversation with a stranger on a bus or train.
- Test drive a new car.
- Read something that inspires you.
- Say no to something.
- Smile at five people you like the look of.
- Write five cards to people in your life expressing your appreciation and gratitude to them.
- Sleep on the beach or in the garden on a warm summer's night.
- Go to the animal home and offer to take a dog out for a walk.
- Cook something absolutely delicious – no ready meals!
- Call a friend or your partner and spontaneously drive to the coast or to the countryside for the evening.
- Put on a favourite tune and sing your heart out or dance along with all your might – alone or with family or friends.
- Go for a long walk, breathing deeply and noticing whatever there is of nature around you.
- Take a bus ride to anywhere.
- Have a relaxing aromatherapy bath.
- Light lots of candles and listen to music that touches your mood.
- Have a night in and make it a completely special time for you to do what you want.

What else can you think of? Get together with friends and see how many ideas you can come up with.

Become a giver as well as a taker

We all give and take at different times in our lives and to varying degrees. When we are single, we can sometimes get quite self-obsessed and focused on ourselves and our own world. Never forget that we are part of a much bigger picture and that there is a great big world out there in which we can make connections and be of service.

Consider what you could do every day to contribute to the world being a better place to be, both for you and for others. Giving in some way, whether simply a smile at the bus driver or money to charity, can really improve our sense of well-being – and you'd be surprised what richness and joy comes in return. So try it out: be playful with this, experiment and observe what difference this makes to how you feel and the way people respond to you. If you make someone's day for them they will want to do the same for someone else, and so it goes on. Doesn't that make the world a much nicer place to live in?

Recognize your needs and get them met

In creating more of a life that you love you are bound to be doing a lot of things that fulfil your needs. But because getting our needs met is an area that we often find challenging, they deserve special attention.

It's not surprising that many of us don't acknowledge our needs, let alone know how to get them met, because we spend a lot of our lives not even being aware that we have them. When we go to school we learn how to read and write and add up, and we learn to conform to routine and discipline. We rarely learn to recognize our own needs, and even if we do, asking for them to be met can be really hard.

The result is that we often adopt ways of getting them met that are not helpful to us or to others. Harry, for example, thought that the only way he would be loved by Julie was to keep her happy (see page 54). If he had remained true to himself, he might have recognized far sooner that he and Julie were not right for each other and would not have been left feeling compromised and bewildered.

What is a need?

Needs describe things that have to be present for us, first, to survive and, second, to be our best. For example, we all have *physical needs* for food, drink and shelter. We also have *emotional needs* for love, acknowledgement and connection.

There is a recognized medical condition in children known as 'failure to thrive' in which, despite having all their physical needs met, the child does not grow or respond energetically to those around him or her. The cause is believed to be related to the amount of loving attention these children receive: it is thought that when this is lacking, the child fails to grow physically and psychologically and may even die.

As adults, we too have emotional needs, and if they are persistently not met then we will feel angry, depressed, stressed and unhappy. We may compensate for this in ways that are not healthy and which can turn into addictions: excessive use of alcohol or caffeine, casual sex, creating dramas in our lives, compulsive shopping, drug abuse or falling into and out of relationships.

All these might distract us from our need in the immediate moment, but they do not genuinely meet it; and when we use the wrong strategy to fulfil a need, the need is liable to get bigger. When this happens, eventually the need becomes dominating and we become 'needy' and draining to be around. Thus, if we don't address our emotional needs we can actually end up pushing people away rather than attracting people who might genuinely meet them.

How do we start to recognize our needs?

In chapter 3 we talked about feelings and how helpful it is to be in touch with our emotions. Being aware of our feelings can really help us understand our needs. In his book *Nonviolent Communication: A Language of Compassion*, Marshall Rosenberg suggests that our feelings are like a temperature gauge by which we can recognize whether or not our needs are being met or not. If we feel angry, sad, frightened or any other negative feeling, this is a sign that our needs are not being met. If we feel joy, happiness or any positive feeling, then this indicates that, at some level, our needs are being met.

Wouldn't it be useful if we could learn to recognize what our needs are and create a healthy set of strategies for getting them met? A 'set' of strategies is best, because then if one stops working, there are other things in our lives that we can fall back on. If our only way to get our need for love met is through our most intimate relationship, then should that relationship end, the gap in our lives will be huge. However, if we have friends and family whom we love and who, in turn, are able to show us love, then – although we are not suggesting it will take away all of the pain – some of our need for love will still be getting met.

Take a look at the list of needs on the following pages, and circle the 10 needs with which you can most readily identify. Be honest with yourself. If you feel embarrassed that something might be a need but you don't want to admit it, then it most probably is!

Needs List

Be Accepted
- Approved
- Permitted
- Welcomed
- Included
- Popular
- Allowed
- Respected
- Sanctioned
- Tolerated

To Accomplish
- Achieve
- Reach
- Yield
- Fulfil
- Profit
- Professional
- Realize
- Attain
- Victory

Be Acknowledged
- Worthy
- Flattered
- Appreciated
- Praised
- Complimented
- Valued
- Honoured
- Prized
- Thanked

Be Loved
- Liked
- Held fondly
- Relished
- Cherished
- Desired
- Touched
- Esteemed
- Preferred
- Adored

Be Right
- Correct
- Morally right
- Supported
- Not mistaken
- Deferred to
- Encouraged
- Honest
- Confirmed
- Understood

Be Cared for
- Get attention
- Saved
- Tenderness
- Helped
- Attended to
- Get gifts
- Cared about
- Treasured
- Embraced

Certainty
- Clarity
- Obviousness
- Commitments
- Accuracy
- Guarantee
- Exactness
- Assurance
- Promises
- Precision

Be Comfortable
- Luxury
- Prosperity
- Not work
- Opulence
- Indulgence
- Taken care of
- Excess
- Abundance
- Served

To Communicate
- Heard
- Make a point
- Listened to
- Gossip
- Share
- Comment
- Tell stories
- Talk
- Informed

To Control
- Dominate
- Manage
- Not ignored
- Command
- Correct others
- Keep status quo
- Restrain
- Obeyed
- Restrict

Be Needed
- Improve others
- Craved
- Need to give
- Be a critical link
- Please others
- Important
- Useful
- Affect others
- Material

Duty
- Obligated
- Obey
- Prove self
- Do the right thing
- Have a task
- Devoted
- Follow
- Satisfy others
- Have a cause

Be Free
- Unrestricted
- Independent
- Not obligated
- Privileged
- Autonomous
- Self-reliant
- Immune
- Supreme
- Liberated

Honesty
- Forthrightness
- Sincerity
- No withholding
- Uprightness
- Loyalty
- No invasions
- No lying
- Frankness
- Tell all

Order
- Perfection
- Sequential
- Rightness
- Pleasing
- Checklists
- Exactness
- Consistent
- Unvarying
- Regulated

Peace
- Quietness
- Reconciliation
- Agreements
- Calmness
- Stillness
- Respite
- Unity
- Balance
- Steadiness

Power
- Authority
- Omnipotence
- Stamina
- Capacity
- Strength
- Privilege
- Results
- Might
- Influence

Recogition
- Noticed
- Regarded well
- Pay attention
- Remembered
- Get credit
- Seen
- Known for
- Acclaim
- Celebrated

Safety
- Security
- Fully informed
- Cautious
- Protected
- Deliberate
- Alert
- Stable
- Vigilant
- Guarded

Work
- Career
- Press, push
- Responsibility
- Performance
- Make it happen
- Industriousness
- Vocation
- A task
- Busy

Source: CoachUniversity – www.coachu.com

Once you've circled your 10 needs, narrow the list down further to your top three needs. To help you prioritize, think about which need, if it were met, would automatically satisfy other needs as well. For example, if my need for *influence* (which comes under power in the needs list) were met then that would also automatically fulfil my need for recognition; so my need to have *influence* is the need that would most benefit from being met.

Once you've prioritized your needs, complete the exercise below, which will help you develop some reliable ways to get each of those needs met.

EXERCISE: GETTING YOUR NEEDS MET

Taking one of your top three needs at a time, answer the following questions, noting your answers in your journal:

- Who am I when this need is met? How do I act? What do I think about? What motivates me?
  Identify three instances from your past when this need has been met. Describe how you felt each time and recall what was happening that contributed to this need being met.
- Who am I when this need is not being met? How do I act? What do I think about? What motivates me?
  Identify three instances from your past when this need has not been met. Again, describe how you felt and recall what was happening or not happening that meant this need was not being met.
- How well is this need being met right now in your life?
- What three changes do you wish to make in your life that will ensure this need is met fully?
- With whom could you share this? Who could support you and ensure you make the changes you want?

The changes you make may be small or large. If they are large, break them down into manageable steps. To get your need for achievement met, for example, you may decide to change jobs; this may take time, and some of the steps might be to redesign your CV or do some extra training. In the meantime, making sure you acknowledge your achievements and goals, and getting other people to do so too will support you in the steps you take and in being successful.

Asking for your needs to be met

Getting our needs met often involves making requests of others, and this may stop us from seeking help. 'I just don't feel comfortable doing this.' 'It doesn't feel real.' 'What if the other person rejects me?' We've heard all these comments and more in our coaching sessions and workshops.

This resistance is understandable; it comes from our self-perception based on our fears and feelings from the past. What happened to us when we were younger, however, may not be relevant for us today. Asking for our needs to be met is like flexing a muscle that we didn't know was there. We feel it's clumsy, awkward, not very strong and are worried it may ache afterwards. So what do we do if we want a muscle to get stronger? We go to the gym and work out, and the more we practise the easier it becomes.

So, if you feel uncomfortable when you first make a request for yourself, accept that this is a stretch, but a very positive stretch in looking after yourself. If you don't feel real or authentic, tell the person to whom you are making the request: 'I feel a bit foolish asking this of you, but this is something important to me…'

The other person does have a right not to accede to your request and it's important to recognize this. However, if your approach is sincere and heartfelt, it's likely you will be able to reach a solution that suits both of you – and who knows what you could achieve?

MARY'S STORY: While my marriage was breaking up I was feeling pretty down and vulnerable, so I looked at my own needs. I recognized that what was lacking at that time in my life was being told how loved I was. I identified three people whom I could ask to keep this need topped up for me. I really did not want to do this at first; I felt foolish and vulnerable asking someone to let me know they loved me.

I eventually plucked up courage and approached two close friends. I asked them both if they could send me a card once a week for the next six weeks and to write in the card what I meant to them as a friend. My first friend willingly agreed and I received a delightful selection of beautiful cards containing her sincere sentiments and thoughts about me. No matter how I was feeling at the time, when each one arrived it always brought a smile to my lips.

My second friend was less comfortable with my request and said she'd prefer to send me regular text messages. I was happy with that and to this day we still regularly send each other loving and appreciative messages, which can really pick me up whatever is happening in my life. My relationship with both my friends is now much closer, more open and real.

The third person I had identified was my father. I know both my parents loved me, but as I'd moved down to London from the north many years before, my most regular contact with them was on the telephone; and most of the time it was my mother I chatted with. My father rarely called me so I wanted to ask him to call me once a week and to tell me he loved me.

Well, when I realized that this was what I wanted, I squirmed and wriggled. How could I ask him? I told myself he might think that I didn't think he loved me, or he might say no, or, even worse, tell me to stop being so silly! I reflected on this and was able to recognize that these were my thoughts and not his: I had no idea what he was really thinking. I called my father and I remember physically shaking as I did so. But you know what? He was delighted that I asked and, as a result, I am now closer not only to him, but also to my mother as we are all now much freer in appreciating and acknowledging our love for one another.

Asking for particular needs to be met can feel like a hard thing to do: first, because we may well be conditioned not to ask for things for ourselves and so it may feel like a selfish thing to do; second, because we tell ourselves all sorts of things about how the person we are asking will feel and react, just as Mary did about her father; third, because it may not feel real for us. All of these things are our fear talking to us.

We would encourage you to be real and authentic both in making your request and in receiving the response. Honesty and truthfulness are the best basis for successful communication within relationships, so this is good practice. If the other person does not feel comfortable, they have the right to refuse or to make another suggestion instead. In Mary's case, one of her friends did not want to send her cards; however, she was happy with texting instead. Negotiating and finding out what feels comfortable for both of you ensures that what you do receive is real and genuine rather than forced and done merely to keep you happy.

Recognizing that you have a strong need for love is important, and it's worth being aware of what you have been doing in order to get that need met. However, a request for love might be too much for some people; so be realistic, and if this seems too much to ask for too soon, try asking for other less emotive needs to be met in ways that will let you know that you are cared for and appreciated.

Despite your reservations and your fears, we strongly recommend you clearly identify your emotional needs and then find ways of getting them met. Having our needs fully met can transform how we feel about ourselves, which impacts greatly on how we act and respond to others and, in turn, how they respond to us.

A word about loneliness

One of the most common points raised by our clients and friends when not in a relationship, and one that we've experienced ourselves, is the feeling of loneliness that arises out of not having a deep, intimate connection with another.

We'd love to be able to say that when you've created a wonderfully fulfilling life for yourself as an independent person you will never feel lonely, but we know that that is not how it is. It's our experience that however good your life is, whether single or shared, you will sometimes feel alone.

When you are single there will be times when it seems that everyone else is celebrating family occasions, or on holiday or out for dinner with friends, and we are not. Or someone promises to call and then doesn't. And so we feel lonely and a bit isolated. We lose the connection with ourselves because we seem to have lost it with others.

Part of taking care of ourselves is to be aware that we might feel like this sometimes, and that this feeling will pass if we try not to deny its existence and instead merely acknowledge it for what it is. It can be helpful to set up a structure that will support us through these times. Make sure there are people you can call if you need to talk; or give yourself permission to hide under the duvet if that is what you want instead. It's OK. We're only human.

Don't forget, having a relationship is not a panacea for loneliness. Both of us and many of our clients have felt loneliest and most disconnected when we have been in a relationship that is wrong for us. If that strikes a chord with you, remember that time – and then remind yourself of what great things you have in your life right now.

Getting your sexual needs met

Sex is not just a very important part of any intimate, loving relationship; for many of us it can be a driving force in our adult lives. So what do we do when we are not in a relationship? How do we get our sexual needs met?

Some people switch off from sex completely. Others sleep with people on a casual basis and need to take the necessary precautions to avoid unwanted pregnancy and sexually transmitted diseases.

You could take a lover. However, if you know that you become easily emotionally involved with someone once you sleep with them, we would not recommend this strategy. If you are able to separate your sexual needs from your emotional ones, are not ready for commitment but have a need for sexual intimacy, then this may work for you; but do take care. The chemicals that mix with our hormones during sex are designed to encourage us to become attached to each other (this applies as much for men as it does for women), so if you are sure your lover is not a person with whom you want to have a long-term relationship then make sure you set really clear limits on how far the relationship can go, such as not seeing each other too often, being very clear you are dating other people and whatever else is important to you.

For many people, these options are not satisfactory; and yet they are aware that something is missing by not having sexual contact.

Is it the need for:

- touch?
- stroking?
- being held?
- passion?
- connection?
- intimacy?
- physical satisfaction?
- communication?

You may be able to think of other things too.

While we acknowledge there is nothing like the intimate touch of a lover, there are ways to get those needs met in other ways. Sensual activities, such as massage and long, luxurious baths, can be a great way to relax and pamper our bodies.

If you are tactile, ensure you have friends or family with whom hugging, touch and affection form a natural part of your relationship. Dancing is a great way to express sexual energy and to really get in touch with our bodies.

Tantra is a spiritual practice that is linked with sexual fulfilment but can offer another way of creating deep and sensual connection with yourself and others without having sex. Tantra classes and courses are held in many areas and you can check these out for yourself. See our list of resources and website on pages 190–92 for more information.

Then there are sex toys. You don't need to be in a relationship in order to play with them. For women who have not tried them out – buy a book on the subject (we recommend a couple of our favourites at the back of this book), find out the difference between a vibrator and a dildo, learn about lubricants and have some fun.

There are lots of specialist books on sex and there are therapists who specialize in dealing with sexual problems, so we have not gone into much detail here. It is important, however, to stress that sex is normal: we all have sexual needs to varying degrees and it is part of everyday life to get those needs met.

Increase your attractiveness

According to the law of attraction, each of us is like a giant magnet, attracting situations that match the energy which we put out into the world; in other words, like attracts like. If we put out negative fearful energy, we attract negative, fearful situations, while positive energy attracts positivity.

We are all attracting all of the time; it's just that sometimes we seem to attract things that we'd really prefer not to. So what might be getting in the way of our attracting what we want into our lives?

To attract more of what you really want there are some very simple principles we can follow; some of them we have already mentioned, others are still to come. But in the meantime here is a summary.

Get rid of the things that drain your energy

Do you have a list of things that you are putting up with? How long is it? As coaches, we refer to these things as 'tolerations'. Tolerations can be large or small, material or emotional.

Ask yourself:
- What in your environment is draining your energy at the moment? Are you overwhelmed with clutter in your life? Is your home so untidy that you feel you can't ask people round? Are you using this as an excuse to keep people away from you?
- What are you putting up with in your relationships? Do you allow people to cancel arrangements they've made with you at short notice for fear of not wanting to rock the boat and possibly losing a friend?

And:
- Make a list of up to 20 things that you are tolerating right now.

We put up with all sorts of things and justify it to ourselves, because often in the short term it is easier. However, in the long term these things literally drain us of our energy.

I might tolerate my cluttered office because in the short term it's more important that I get other jobs done first. But in the long-term my cluttered office is going to inhibit my ability to be efficient and will drain my energy whenever I have to find something.

In relationships, some people tolerate their partners shouting at them because they are scared they will cause more trouble by asking them to talk in a calm voice. However, the more you put up with being spoken to in that way, the more you are allowing your motivation and self-esteem to be eroded, to the detriment of the relationship, of the people around you and of yourself. In chapter 8 we will look at ways in which you can handle tolerations in your relationship.

Do more things that give you energy

We talked earlier about surrounding yourself with people who support you and with whom you feel most comfortable. Both of these things give you energy.

It is also important that you have healthy activities in your life that help you to express yourself and make you feel totally fulfilled. Some people find this in their work. Not only are they energized, but they receive financial reward, too. It's important to retain balance, however, because losing yourself in your work can mean you are avoiding other things in your life. We suggest that, if you haven't done so already, you find an activity you can do regularly which inspires, motivates and energizes you.

Think about it:
- What do you really love to do?
- What activity do you lose yourself in? Where does time disappear for you?
- When and where do you have lots of energy? Alternatively, when and where do you notice that your energy is low?
- What can you take from your observations and what action are you going to take to ensure you have activities in your life you are passionate about?

Raise your standards and set clear boundaries

We talked about Louise on page 64 and about how she used affirmations to help empower herself to set a limit to her boyfriend's teasing behaviour. In her past, Louise would have put up with being teased. However, she knew she was looking for a mutually respectful relationship and so she set a standard for what behaviour fitted with what she wanted and what didn't.

Having this standard and setting a boundary around it helped her recognize when it wasn't being met and the boundary was being crossed. With this awareness she was able to make a choice: she chose to let go of a relationship that she felt would not be good for her.

As we stop tolerating unacceptable behaviour from people who show us no regard and, instead, raise our standards to hold out for what we want, we start to attract the right sort of people into our lives – people who only want the best for us and who treat us with love and respect. And so we turn a vicious cycle into a virtuous cycle.

Get clear about what you want and get excited about it

In her book *Excuse Me, Your Life Is Waiting*, Lynn Grabhorn offers a very simple process for attracting what you want into your life:

- *Get clear about what you don't want.* This frees you up to focus on the things that matter to you.
- *State what it is you do want.* State this in the positive, for example: 'I want a job that has variety and allows me to meet new people.'
- *Get excited and positively emotional about it.* Really get in touch with the feelings you associate with achieving what it is you want.
- Expect, listen and allow it to happen.

The third point is crucial. The more we engage with positive emotions, the more we open up and send out positive energy. Remember, like attracts like: if you are sending out positive energy, you will receive positive energy back, which means that you will attract more positive people and positive experiences to you.

Are you getting in your own way?

Usually, what gets in the way of creating what we want in our life and relationships is ourselves. When we were brainstorming ideas for the content of this book, if one of us started to get slightly negative, the other would use a catchphrase, such as 'get out of your own way' or 'get over yourself', and we would immediately laugh and lighten up.

This was a great reminder that it is usually our own self-limiting beliefs that get in our way, causing us to view the world from a particular perspective. Someone else, with a different history and another belief system, would have a completely different view of the world and would probably hold different beliefs from ours. So, which set of beliefs is true? Well, there is not simply one truth but many, and we can modify our beliefs. It is worth sometimes trying to create a different reality for ourselves by practising seeing the world through different eyes.

MARY'S STORY: At one point, I was working with a group whom I perceived to be very challenging, particularly one participant who consistently took a contrary view and was critical and dismissive of the answers and ideas the group came up with.

I talked this through with a colleague, who noticed that I was focusing all my attention and energy on this one specific person. My colleague suggested that I change the filter through which I was looking at the group members and try reframing the situation by being open to all the positive things that were going on in the group.

Next time I did just that; and not only did I enjoy working with the group much more, but everyone worked together more effectively – including the person who had previously been so critical.

Your action plan for creating a life you love

In completing this chapter you will have reflected on many things in your life, and we hope it will have brought to light some of the ways in which you can ensure you have a fulfilling life whether you are in a relationship or not. Thinking about these things is not enough. What will make the real difference is taking action.

Yet, it's often at the time of taking action that we can make all sorts of excuses to ourselves that will keep us safely in our comfort zone. This is a time of choice: to either keep doing things the same or to take a step in a different direction, a step that may well stretch and challenge you. It doesn't have to be a huge step, but it does help for it to be a step that enables you to create a life and future that is different to your past and from which there is no turning back.

Steffi's Story

Steffi was getting over the break up of a long-term relationship and was feeling like she was in a rut. Work was ticking over, but she felt understimulated. She had a good social life with her friends, but she was still down about the end of her relationship, which had happened nine months earlier.

When she reviewed her life with her coach, Steffi recognized that many of the activities she'd done in her life were all in connection with her partner and that there was little that she did independently. She took a look at what the things were she really loved to do and realized she adored travel and adventure and since the break up had done very little. However, at this time in her life Steffi really depended on her friends for support and didn't want to leave them. So, despite dreaming about taking time off and going travelling she kept booking things in her diary that stopped her from taking the plunge.

Eventually, after another three months of feeling like she wasn't going anywhere, Steffi realized she could stay where she was or she could do something to make a difference. She asked her boss if she could take a sabbatical and, despite feeling fearful, she took the plunge and bought a round-the-world air ticket. Her fear didn't go away, but once she'd made the commitment through the purchase of her ticket, she had to take action to make her trip happen. As her plans took shape her fear began to recede and was replaced by excitement.

She took her trip, met loads of new people, and even had a couple of short-term relationships, and returned with renewed confidence about herself and her future.

So what are the things small or large, you are going to commit yourself to doing? Answer the questions in the exercise below to help you create an action plan for a great life.

EXERCISE: ACTION PLAN FOR A GREAT LIFE

- What affirmation will remind you what a great person you are?
- What areas in your life do you want to change or improve?
- How committed are you to making these changes?
- What's stopping you?
- What's missing for you?
- When you imagine making the changes, how energized do you feel?
- What steps will you take and what time limit will you give yourself?
- What can you do to ensure you take these steps?
- Who will you ask to support you in your actions?
- What rewards will you give yourself for each step you achieve?

To laugh often and much; to win the respect of intelligent people and affection of children; to earn the appreciation of honest critics and endure the betrayal of false friends; to appreciate beauty, to find the best in others; to leave the world a bit better, whether by a healthy child, a garden patch, or a redeemed social condition; to know even one life has breathed easier because you have lived. This is to have succeeded.

Ralph Waldo Emerson

5

Knowing What You Really Want

> *Choose your life's mate carefully. From this one decision will come ninety percent of all your happiness or misery.*

From *Life's Little Instruction Book* by H. Jackson Brown Jr

Having completed the exercises from the previous chapters you will now have a greater understanding of who you truly are, what it is you need in order to be your best and the importance of taking steps to lead a fulfilling life with or without a partner.

We hope that you will be feeling more confident about yourself and able to appreciate what a great person you are – someone who is worth getting to know, who is attractive (we're talking about personality here, not just looks) – and that whoever is fortunate to have you as their partner is going to be very lucky.

The reason we place so much emphasis on you having a positive sense of self-worth is that if you want to create a relationship that really works for you, then you must believe you deserve this. We are at the point now where we are hoping that you are able to own your strengths and personal power. It is going to be up to you to set out clearly what it is you really want in a relationship and to go out and get it.

What we really want for you is to be the chooser in your relationships and in life, rather than sitting on the sidelines waiting to be chosen and then feeling grateful just because you have been.

This is the opportunity for you to become clear about what it is you want in and from your intimate relatikonship. From clarity comes the power for you to be discerning when meeting potential partners.

> **By the end of the chapter we hope you will have:**
> - a much clearer understanding of the sort of relationship you want and deserve to have;
> - learned what it is you truly value in life, in order to have a life where you feel fulfilled and at peace;
> - created your top five essential relationship requirements that are in line with your values;
> - understood the difference between co-dependence, independence and interdependence, and chosen the kind of relationship you are seeking now;
> - a clear vision of the ideal life you are looking to create with your partner.

Are you ready for this?

We know from experience that it's important to be aware of how 'ready' you actually are, as this will affect the type of relationship you might want to have and the sort of partner you attract.

In chapter 3 we looked at getting to know and love ourselves from the inside out, and in chapter 4 we developed strategies that would support us in the creation of a great life for ourselves, whether in a relationship or not. We did this because both self-awareness and the development of personal resources are key to being able to reach true independence. Why is being independent so important? Well, it is a sign that we are taking responsibility in all areas of our lives. If we are physically, intellectually, emotionally and financially independent then we are not looking for a relationship to fill the gaps for us. This makes us less vulnerable to choosing someone who might not be the best option for us in the long term.

Simon's Story

Simon always had to be in a relationship. He never felt like a complete person on his own. As a child, he had never felt good enough for his parents and he was constantly trying to find ways to make them love him more. When his school report showed an A, they wanted to know why he had not got an A+. When he proudly gave them a painting he had made at school, they criticized the standard of the teaching that allowed such substandard work.

It seemed that his younger brother was indulged where he was not, and whatever the younger boy did was more extraordinary, more amusing, more entertaining and more creative. So, Simon felt unloved and, indeed, unlovable.

So strong, yet not met was Simon's need for love that he continued to seek it as an adult by going from one relationship to the next. He could not bear to be on his own and his choice of partner was usually based on how receptive that person was to him.

He had a series of relationships that varied in length, some lasting weeks, some for years, but there was never any gap in between. When one ended, he would quickly move on to the next one. His partners would at first feel flattered, as he would shower them with poetry and gifts and they would respond by giving him the love and attention he craved. But when the relationship settled down into something approaching normality and the first flush of romance had passed, Simon could not bear it if he was not constantly being reminded by his partner how much she loved him. He would become demanding and accusing, and invariably his partners felt overwhelmed by his constant need for attention. One by one, his relationships fell apart. The pattern had been set and Simon had no idea how he was contributing to it.

From dependence to interdependence

> *Two halves don't make a whole, but two whole people make a relationship.*
>
> Kim Cattrall

In his book *The Seven Habits of Highly Effective People*, Stephen Covey describes our journey to maturity from *dependence*, through *independence*, to *interdependence*.

When we are first born, we are completely dependent on others for our survival. We rely on them for food, love, care and safety.

As we grow and develop, we learn to feed ourselves and develop ways of conducting relationships that work for us. We move towards some level of independence. We are not fully independent, however, because the way we learn to relate in our early years will often be a survival strategy, so that we may well learn to give up on some part of ourselves and our own needs in order to receive love.

Co-dependence

If we have not become aware of these unsatisfied needs, we tend unconsciously to seek a partner who can help us get them met in a relationship. What often happens is that we attract and are attracted to a partner whose needs complement our own. And so we fit together like the pieces in a jigsaw puzzle and we develop what is known as a *co-dependent* relationship. So on our route from *dependence* to *independence* we get diverted into *co-dependence*.

What's wrong with co-dependence, you might ask? In many ways a co-dependent relationship may work; indeed, it is the traditional model for marriages, where the wife stays at home to look after the children and the husband goes to work in order to earn money for the family. Traditionally, many women look for a husband who provides and many men simply want an attractive woman who will look after them. Each needs the other, either to feel safe and protected or to boost their self-esteem. It can work, but in today's society, where independence and equality are more greatly valued, co-dependence is becoming more and more outmoded.

Betty's Story

Betty feared learning to drive and was thus totally reliant on her husband to take her anywhere she had to go. She never really had to address this fear as she always had her husband to take her around. She loved the attention he gave her; she was his precious little princess. In turn, he felt appreciated and valued by Betty. Her dependence upon him to look after her fulfilled his need to be in control, something he had never felt as a boy growing up.

Betty and her husband weren't consciously aware of their co-dependence. Each of them had taken up their respective roles within the relationship, and it was a pattern that would continue to work provided the relationship was not being challenged. However, such a co-dependent relationship can also support unhelpful and potentially damaging behaviour.

A classic situation is when one partner puts up with and accepts the other's drinking habits, violent behaviour or repeated infidelity. Perhaps they stay in the relationship in the constant hope that the problem will eventually go away and that their partner will turn into the loving person that they may occasionally have glimpsed in the past. You may see indications of these relationships in a working context, where the boss shouts irrationally at an employee who tolerates this for fear of losing their job.

EXERCISE: BEWARE OF CO-DEPENDENCE

Simply start noticing where people might be acting in a co-dependent way. Do you think you do it? Do people that you know do it? The more you observe, the more you will be aware, and this will put you in a better position to make the choices that are right for you.

Independence and interdependence

For a relationship to flourish, it is really important to work on yourself from the inside out, by understanding what your needs are and by taking responsibility for getting them met. If we do this, then we mature and become *independent*, and once we are fully independent we can then choose whether we want to be *interdependent*.

An interdependent relationship is one where each person is able to maintain a sense of themselves. They do not rely on the other person to make them feel good, although they will appreciate their own and the other person's needs and will work together in an open and conscious way to ensure both parties get their needs met.

Sara and Jonathon's Story

Sara felt great about herself and yet still had a need to be cherished. As an independent person she had a circle of friends whose attention, compliments and confirmation of her strengths met this need.

When she first met Jonathon she felt that one thing that was missing was the feeling of being cherished by him. She had a need for him to recognize and value her qualities. Despite getting this need met outside of the relationship, she still wanted a partner who would be prepared to give her this type of attention.

She asked Jonathon if he would be willing to do this, and he agreed to give it a go. Sara, too, was willing to fulfil the needs that Jonathon had, but neither was overly reliant on the other to do this exclusively for them. When they began to meet each other's expressed needs, the relationship went from strength to strength.

Stephen Covey uses simple language to describe each stage in this maturity spectrum, and this provides a useful way of recognizing at what stage of dependence we are at a particular time:

- Dependence is illustrated by 'you': 'You will look after me', 'You are to blame for what happened'.
- Independence is illustrated by 'I': 'I did it for myself', 'I am responsible', 'I have choices'.
- Interdependence is illustrated by 'we': 'We do things better together', 'We are cooperative'.

Just be aware

Going from dependence to independence through to interdependence is something that happens over time, and we're not advising against entering a relationship until you can act in a fully interdependent way. Quite the opposite, in fact. It's pretty hard to reach maturity without life experience, and in order to move from dependence to interdependence it is necessary to engage in experiences from which we learn.

It is also quite likely that there will be some areas in our lives where we are more independent than others. For example, I might well be able to fend for myself physically and intellectually; I can look after myself and think my own thoughts; but I might still need other people's approval of me to feel alright. If this is akin to your situation, there is nothing wrong with this. People who have achieved success in all areas of their lives still have needs relating to approval and love.

What is important is to be aware of where you are on the spectrum and how this will influence the type of relationship and partner you may attract. You may want to address your own dependence or even independence (which can become its own form of self-protection against having a relationship) before you actually seek a relationship.

EXERCISE: DEPENDENCE–INTERDEPENDENCE SPECTRUM

The table opposite is designed to help you become aware of where you are now on the dependence–interdependence spectrum. Tick the statements that apply to you and see in which column most of them go.

Reviewing your choices will allow you to see what it is you are expecting from a relationship overall. If you feel that your relationships are still too needy and dependent and you would like them to be more interdepndent, then we suggest you refer back to chapters 2, 3 and 4 or seek the guidance of a relationship coach to do some further work. If you feel ready, then read on.

What sort of relationship are you looking for?

From very early on in our lives we are led to believe that a long-term committed relationship between two people who live together and have children is the thing to aim for. This is reinforced by images in the media and generally is the 'norm' in our society.

However, just because this is what most people do, it does not mean that it is right for everybody, and there are many different ways that people can have loving and fulfilling relationships without conforming to this model.

The trend in modern society is away from this traditional view of the family. It is now widely accepted that there are many other, different ways in which people can have loving and fulfilling relationships.

DEPENDENCE	INTERDEPENDENCE
I want a partner to:	*I want a partner to:*
☐ make my life complete.	☐ give and receive love.
☐ give me financial security.	☐ contribute to our overall financial security.
☐ solve my problems.	
☐ make difficult decisions for me.	☐ work out problems together.
☐ make me feel sexually fulfilled.	☐ consult with me.
☐ look after all the paperwork.	☐ develop a sexually fulfilling life we both enjoy.
☐ make me feel good about myself.	
☐ define who I am.	☐ join in planning and sharing.
☐ make me feel included.	☐ acknowledge my needs.
☐ do all the housework and organizing round the home.	☐ contribute to both of ours emotional security.
☐ bring in the money.	☐ have pursuits separate to my own.
☐ nurture and feed me.	☐ listen to me when I ask for support.
☐ look good on my arm.	☐ negotiate with me on how we might meet each other's needs.
☐ agree with me.	
☐ blindly support me even when they might not agree with me.	☐ know what they want and ask for this.
	☐ challenge me when I am mistaken.
☐ laugh at all my jokes.	☐ build on each others ideas.
☐ provide me with a good social life.	☐ share laughter and joy.
☐ look after the kids.	☐ share different perspectives.
☐ cook all my meals for me.	☐ hold me when I ask.

Zoë's Story

Zoë was divorced after a very unhappy marriage in which she had remained because she thought she 'should' and didn't want to disappoint her parents. Since her divorce, other things in Zoë's life had become just as important to her as having a relationship, and although she did want a long-term partner, she knew she required a lot of personal time and space alone and that, therefore, for the foreseeable future, living with someone again was not an option.

Zoë came to see that the sort of relationship that would make her happy would be one where she and a partner always kept a high degree of independence and separateness. She felt liberated and excited by this insight, whereas before she had almost been ignoring this part of her life because she had had a fixed view of the sort of relationship that might be available to her.

Open yourself up to the options that are out there in terms of the sort of relationship you want.

- How much time do you want to devote to a relationship?
- How intense do you want the relationship to be?
- Are you ready to commit to an exclusive relationship?
- Do you envisage living with someone eventually or would you prefer to keep homes separate?
- Are you interested in a relationship that is local or long-distance?
- Do you just want some interim fun or do you want to build a life with someone?

Pattie's Story

Pattie separated from her husband a couple of years ago and during the past six months had started to date again. She was seeking a long-term relationship but was also aware of how much she missed physical contact with a man. So, when she met someone through a dating agency to whom she felt very sexually attracted but with whom she realized she had little in common, she told him she would not be seeing him again and explained her reasons.

This led to her date admitting that he was not really looking for a long-term relationship at this stage as he was only recently out of his marriage and was not ready to think about committing to the future. With this out in the open they felt free to admit their attraction for each other and decided to explore the relationship further, with a view to it becoming a sexual one with no strings attached.

And that is what it became, with both Pattie and her lover getting certain needs met while she continued her search for a life partner. Having a lover took the pressure off Pattie's search for a committed relationship and meant she was less likely to enter one for the wrong reasons. What she was prepared to commit to, however, was sexual exclusivity, and she expected the same from her lover.

Consider what your needs are and which needs you would like a relationship to fulfil. Pattie's way of getting her immediate needs met might not suit everyone, but it can work for some people. It is important to be clear about what you are seeking (we will go into this later) and to be able to articulate this, because although it is not up to you to take responsibility for other people's feelings, it is not your job to hurt people either. If you are open and honest, then they have choices.

Consider, also, at what stage your life is. You may want to settle down and have a family; or perhaps you have done all that and are on the second or third time around, with needs and desires quite different from those you had earlier. You may also have to take into account children from your own or your partner's previous relationships, who will add joys and challenges of their own.

If you are recently out of a relationship you may want to explore and have two or three relationships before you decide to settle down again. Many people have what is known as a transitional relationship after a serious long-term relationship breaks up, and this can provide both parties with an opportunity to heal and to recover a positive sense of themselves.

What's important to you in terms of how you live your life?

As well as getting clear about where you are at in your life and the sort of relationship that would work best for you, it is helpful to take some time to look at your personal values.

Values are like the benchmarks by which we make decisions on what works or doesn't work for us. When we live in accordance with our values, we feel fulfilled. For example, if one of your values is equality, then you would find it very hard to be in a relationship where your partner expected you to do something he was not prepared to do himself, or where you did not share things equally.

The more you live your life in tune with your values, then the more at peace you will be. Acting with integrity, rather than pulling in different directions, you will maximize your natural energy – which, as you will recall from the last chapter, will add to your personal attraction!

Values offer a benchmark for establishing whether or not you are in a relationship that works for you. A lack of shared values can lead to arguments and misunderstandings, and the feeling that one or other of you is compromising your integrity. We believe that a shared vision of what you want your life together to look like, along with shared values, are fundamental to the success of any relationship.

Take a look at the next exercise and complete at least two of the sections to help you understand what your values are. The values that are most central to you are the ones that will come up repeatedly. At the end of the exercise you should be able to identify your top five values.

EXERCISE: YOUR VALUES
WHAT IS CORE TO WHO YOU ARE?

Think about yourself moving into the autumn or winter of your life; imagine reaching quite an old age.

- What do you see yourself still being compelled to do?
- What is so fundamental to you that you cannot not do it?

You may identify practical activities, e.g. doing the garden, or you may think of inner qualities, e.g. caring about others. Then ask yourself:

- Why is doing this so important to you?

This last question is designed to identify the value you place on these fundamental activities or qualities.

STORIES FROM YOUR LIFE

Identify two or three projects or achievements you have completed in your life that gave you a real sense of satisfaction and fulfilment. They can be from any period or area of your life, e.g. school, work, leisure, relationships, etc.

- In your journal, write down your story of each of these achievements, what you did, how you did it.
- Review each story separately and, as you read, consider what was it about this achievement that gave you the satisfaction/ fulfilment. This may bring out some values straight away.
- To go deeper, ask yourself 'Why is this so important to me?' and 'What else makes it so important?'
- Having checked through each story, review the values that have emerged. It is likely that any that are repeated will be core values.

ANGER AND PASSION

Consider:

- What things make you angry?
- What is it about those things that annoy you?
- Why is that important to you?

For example, I get angry and frustrated when I see or hear of people being treated unfairly. I get annoyed because I think everyone has a right to fair treatment. This is important to me because I value fairness and equality.

- What do you find yourself getting passionate about?
- Why do you feel passionate about this?
- Why is that important to you?

For example, I get passionate about certain pieces of music. The reason I do so is because some music hits a chord with me emotionally and helps me release my feelings. What I value here is connection and expressiveness.

SYMBOLS AND METAPHOR

One way to identify how we are living our lives in line with our values is to look at our environment and the physical symbols or metaphors around us. Select a material item that you truly love and that brings you great pleasure. How does this item fit with who you are? What qualities does it possess that fit with your personal values?

For example, I love my car and have done from the day I got it. I feel it fits perfectly with who I am and what I stand for. Why? I bought it second-hand, so that fitted with the value I place on recycling. It's a cabriolet, so the roof comes down and I can connect with fresh air and sunshine. It's quite fast, so it's fun to drive. It took unleaded fuel at a time when this was quite a new thing, so it was less harmful to the environment. It has four seats, so I can easily take passengers. The values it holds for me are mutual caring, fun, responsibility, connection and support.

THE TOP FIVE VALUES

Now try to establish a list of your top five values, as well as the top five that you would be important for you to share with a partner and note both lists in your journal. The lists may contain different values.

Requirements for your relationship

First be clear about what you don't want

Ask yourself what you want from a relationship and you might find you come up with a list of all the things you know you *don't* want. So now is the opportunity to get off your chest all the things you didn't appreciate about your previous relationships. Take out your journal and reflect on those relationships.

For each relationship, note down:
- What were the things you really disliked about that partner?
- How did you feel when the relationship failed?
- Whom or what did you blame?
- What got on your nerves?
- What are the things you definitely do not want repeated in future relationships?

You will end up with a comprehensive list of what you don't want. You might choose to keep this list to remind you; or you might decide to rip it up or burn it, in order to let go of all these negative recollections that you might be holding about your relationships.

Now let's move on to the even more important topic of what it is you do want.

Developing your requirements

We are about to do one of the most important exercises that you can possibly do for finding your soulmate. It is very simple and yet it's amazing how few people do it before entering into a relationship. Those who have done it say it has transformed their lives by enabling them to know what they want from a relationship and then to go out and attract just what they are looking for.

Requirements are like a list of criteria that are based on your personal values and needs, which you can use to help you make decisions about whether someone would be the sort of partner with whom you could happily and lovingly live your ideal life.

Why is it important to have some requirements?

If you were to buy a new car you would probably think about what sort you wanted, the size of engine, the comfort and convenience of the interiors and the price you wanted to pay. Similarly, if you were going to employ someone, it's unlikely you'd take the first person who walked in off the street. In both cases, you would think about what you wanted and probably set out a list of specific things you were looking for.

Yet, often when we meet someone with whom we end up having a relationship, we don't even think about whether they match our needs or values; we often base our decision on physical attraction, sexual chemistry and the experience of how we feel in the moment.

While wanting a partner who is physically attractive to us and with whom we feel good is a must for most of us, it's also important to take into account how our potential partner can contribute to fulfilling our needs and how we want to live our lives.

Creating a clear set of requirements along these lines not only helps us make a decision about whether someone is right for us or not, it also makes it easier to find them – and for them to find us, too, as our clarity increases our attraction. Returning to our car analogy, if you decide the car that fits your criteria is a yellow Mini, then you may notice that you suddenly start seeing an awful lot of yellow Minis on the road. If we've identified what's important to us, we automatically concentrate on those things – almost as if we programme ourselves to tune into a particular waveband and tune out everything else.

EXERCISE: WHAT ARE YOUR REQUIREMENTS?

In your journal, note down all the things you are looking for in a mate. We are assuming that you would want your partner to be free from alcohol and drug addiction, but, if that has been a particular issue for you in the past, then put it down as it is obviously something you need to watch out for.

We are also assuming that you would want your future partner to be physically attractive to you – but beware of specifying exactly what you want them to look like. Kissable lips or blonde hair might be very nice, but will not guarantee that you will feel happy, loved or fulfilled within the relationship. And isn't that what this is all about?

Note down the qualities you are looking for in your ideal relationship with your ideal mate. Use some of the words on the opposite page to help you get started. It's important that you also come up with your own qualities, which are specific to your needs and values. Aim to get down as many qualities as you can. Think not only about what you want your partner to be like, but also about the sorts of experiences you'd like to share. For example, if you have a need to share deep conversations, you may be seeking a partner who is insightful.

• generous	• playful	• intelligent	• energetic
• adventurous	• sensual	• funny	• passionate
• self-aware	• affectionate	• open	• respects my space
• well-read	• sociable	• independent	• good dress sense
• travels	• insightful	• active	• open-minded
• sharer	• practical	• wise	• spontaneous
• loves dogs	• curious	• proactive	• spiritual
• adventurous	• enjoys music	• sociable	• financially secure
• fit	• responsible	• independent	• good cook
• peaceful	• vegetarian	• creative	• wants children
• artistic	• emotionally	• intelligent	• lacking ego
• good listener	• listens	• outgoing	• fun

Also, ask yourself why you are looking for the particular qualities that you seek. Is it to fill a gap in your own life? If so, do not continue, instead please turn back the pages and reread the first four chapters! Or are these qualities that you yourself bring to the relationship and that you want to share with someone?

We are not suggesting that you will want to share all the same activities. But the short-term attraction of opposites does not always bode well for a successful life partnership. The differences that we often tend to overlook in the first excitement of a new relationship can and often do become sources of irritation in the long term.

What we're doing here is looking at what is important for you to have in a relationship so that you feel fully alive and connected to another person, in order that you don't sell out on yourself merely for the sake of having a partner.

Prioritizing your requirements

We are going to be looking at whether your requirements are essential, important or desirable; so, once you've established as many require-ments as possible, the next stage in the process is to start prioritizing.

- First, put a star against your top ten.
- Then, once you've established your top ten, prioritize further by circling your top five requirements.

These final five are your *essential requirements* and they represent the most important things that you require a potential partner to have. These are the criteria by which you make the decision as to whether or not to continue in a relationship – the 'deal breakers', if you like. If they are not present, then the deal is off. We suggest you keep your essential requirements to five. Any more than that and it can become very dif-ficult to tell if someone matches up to what you really want or not.

When you move on to chapters 6 and 7, which are about dating and testing, these are the requirements that are going to guide you, so do make sure they are the things that are most important to you.

How do your essential requirements show up?

To help you get really clear about what it is you are looking for, it's important to specify what it is you mean exactly. So how would these requirements show up for you in reality? Take a look at each of your requirements and ask yourself, if this requirement were present:

- How would your partner be behaving?
- What sort of things would be happening in your relationship?
- How would you be feeling?
- What would you and your partner share together?
- If all your other essential requirements were being met, but not this one, would you still want this relationship? That is, is this requirement negotiable?

If the answer to the last question is 'yes', then perhaps the requirement of discussion is important but not essential. Notice the distinction between the two: essential requirements are non-negotiable.

For example, let's take 'insightful' as an essential requirement. If you met someone who had this quality you would see it showing up in their behaviour, through their ability to talk about themselves in a candid way, to use the experiences they are having to grow and learn, and to be open about themselves and who they are. In your relationship it would be easy to have open conversations about your experiences and you would feel relaxed and secure. You would share an understanding of where each other was coming from. If a partner met all your other requirements but did not meet this one, you could not entertain a relationship with them. This requirement is not negotiable.

Now, take each of your five essential requirements through the questions listed at the bottom of the opposite page, and be as specific as you can be. The more specific you are, the easier it is to find firm evidence as to whether a person matches what it is you looking for.

Important and desirable requirements

The remaining five requirements that you starred in your original list are your *important requirements*. These are the things that are important to you but about which, unlike your essential requirements, you are prepared to be flexible. If they are not present this may cause you some concern and be grounds for future tension; still, there may be room for negotiation and compromise. You know you could live with this requirement being met outside of the relationship.

For example, if you were keen on physical fitness you might like a partner with whom you could play sport or go to the gym. However, there might be other factors that are more important to you than this, and although it would be great if you met someone with this interest, you could always go to the gym with friends instead.

But be warned! If there is no room for negotiation, then you're talking about an essential requirement. It may be essential for you not to share your life with a couch potato, but you may choose to accept that your partner might prefer football rather than going to the gym.

The remaining qualities that you chose at first, but neither circled nor starred, are what we call your *desirable requirements*. It is great if they are present, but it is not a disaster if they are not – they are neither essential nor important.

For example, you may have concerns about money and be seeking someone who must at the very least be financially *responsible* (essential requirement) and should preferably be financially *independent* (important). If they were a multi-millionaire that would be very nice (desirable) – but that would just be a bonus.

Check the rest of your remaining requirements. Are they the cherries on the cake or do you see them more as basic ingredients? If you suspect the latter, you may wish to re-prioritize.

Keeping your list up to date

You now have a list of essential, important and desirable requirements. Remember, it is the essential ones that will be the real guides in your selection of a mate, so pay most attention to these.

You may find that, as you meet different people, different requirements come up for you, and you will want to keep updating your list. Fine: it does not have to be cast in stone. The more you look at it and focus on what it is you really want, the more easily you will know when the right person comes along; and, just as important, you will not move into relationships that could cause you heartache in the end.

ARIANA'S STORY: One of my requirements is self-awareness and I began seeing someone whom I was thrilled to find was incredibly self-aware. However, after several outings it became clear that he was very serious and lacked the playfulness I was also looking for. I was so enamoured of this man's self-awareness it took me some time to appreciate that we didn't laugh much. But once I noticed, I really noticed, and it was a clear indication for me to end the relationship.

What about your potential partner's requirements?

You may well meet someone you like who has not done this sort of self-investigative work and who, although they too will have requirements, may have no idea what these requirements are. So, we suggest that as part of the 'getting to know you' process, you start talking about them.

- What didn't work for your partner in previous relationships?
- What might they be looking for now?
- Why did their past relationships fail?
- Are they repeating a pattern with you, or are they on the rebound?
- What will it take them to resolve the issues of their past?

The sooner you become aware of whether either of you will meet each other's requirements or not, the easier it is to make a decision about whether this is a relationship worth pursuing. Think about it – if you had 'adventurous' as one of your essential requirements, you might want that person to be outgoing, an explorer who loved travelling and getting to know the world. If it turned out that whoever you were seeing preferred to spend all their holidays asleep on the beach, then you would know this was a relationship you would not want to take forward. And it works both ways.

EXERCISE: CREATING A VISION OF YOUR LIFE AND FUTURE RELATIONSHIP

A vision is a big picture of how you want your life to be: a life that honours all your values, your requirements and your needs. Before anything is created (think about the first car, the first television, the first spacecraft) it has first to be imagined and then committed to paper or to some sort of model. Now is your chance to be your own creator.

In chapter 4 you began the process of creating a vision for yourself by developing strategies for living a great life, whether in a relationship or not. Now, we'd like you to take a practical approach to visualizing what your ideal relationship is going to be like. You are going to be creating a collage, so you may want to set aside a few hours to give yourself the opportunity to create a vision of your future life that is really compelling. Before you do this activity you will need:

- a photograph of yourself looking really happy;
- a collection of magazines and pictures for you to choose from;
- a large piece of paper, preferably pink or purple in colour to symbolize love;
- felt-tip pens, again preferably pink, purple or red, but make sure they're visible on the paper.

If you want to, you can do this activity along with a friend, as it can be very validating to share each other's visions.

If you can, record the paragraph below and the questions that follow on tape, so that you can really get into the experience while you're following the steps. If you can't, then maybe put on some gentle music while you read the words to yourself and think of your answers:

Close your eyes and take yourself into your future. Imagine you have met and created your ideal relationship. Take a really good look at what you have created. Get a crystal-clear picture of what is happening. What can you see? What sort of things are you saying to each other? What other sounds do you hear? How is all of this making you feel? Consider the questions and really get in touch with the sights, sounds and feelings that come up for you.

- What sort of person is your partner?
- Do they remind you of anyone? Someone in your network of friends or in the media gaze?
- What qualities do they possess?
- How are they responding to you?
- What activities are you sharing?
- What sorts of things do you discuss?
- How are you dealing with things everyday?

- What is your sex life like?
- How are you sorting out your differences?
- What are you doing together to have fun?
- How are you managing the other relationships in your lives?
- What is happening in your life overall?

Now open your eyes and write down what you experienced and what it is you want in your ideal life and relationship.

Next, look through the magazines and find images that represent how you envisage your ideal partner, as well as the activities and life you would like to be engaging in together. Be as specific as possible. If you want to go trekking in the Himalayas with this person, then find a picture of people travelling together and write next to this: 'We go trekking in the Himalayas together.'

Build up a collage that represents the life you have visualized for yourself. When you have finished, step back and take a look. What can you start creating for yourself now, whether you are with a partner or not? (Remember, living a life you love will not only make you feel great but will increase your powers of attraction.) Place your vision somewhere you will see it every day to remind you of what it is you really want and allow yourself to get gently pulled in its direction.

What next?

If you have completed the exercises in this chapter, you will now be much clearer about what you are looking for in a relationship. And you should have an inspiring vision for the sort of life you'd like to share with a partner. Armed with this clarity, it's now time to start getting out there and meeting people!

If grass can grow through concrete, then love can find you at any time in your life.

Cher, actress and singer (b. 1946)

6

Dating

> *Opportunity dances with those who are*
> *already on the dance floor.*

H. Jackson Brown Jr, author of *Life's Little Instruction Book*

Unless you get out into that big wide world, the chances of your finding your ideal mate are going to be very slim indeed. If you want to meet Mr or Ms Right, you need to find ways of getting out and getting some practice.

This chapter is for you whether or not you are currently single. Obviously, not all of it will apply if you are actually in a committed relationship. But part of the essence of having a great relationship, apart from good communication, companionship and great sex, is to have fun. Who says that dating should stop once you are together? How might your relationship benefit by reintroducing this element into it?

We say reintroducing on the assumption that you will have dated when you first met your partner. And yet, when Ariana used to counsel couples for Relate, one of the things that became apparent to her was that many couples who had got together at an early age had missed out on the dating and flirting stages altogether. When she introduced to them the idea of making dates with each other, they saw new and endless possibilities for having fun together.

There are some definite dos and don'ts around dating which we will go into during this chapter. Being aware of these will help you make conscious decisions about the people you meet. We know that you're not always going to follow them; sometimes caution is thrown to the wind and the rule book gets thrown out of the ou make dating

…hem in mind.

u will have

…fun and flirtatious

…rent types of place where you

…er;

…roactive and the chooser in relation-

s…

- becon… …re of how we can distort the way we view
somebou… …e early stages of a relationship;
- found out how to maintain momentum after you've been rejected;
- become aware of what actually happens when two people feel
the 'chemistry' between them.

Some useful approaches to dating

Dating is an important beginning to a successful relationship. It can offer truly rich experiences, including the opportunity to meet new and interesting people, so that on your way to finding your ideal mate you can make some great friends. It requires you to have a lot of patience, as well as openness towards learning and personal growth.

Practise being yourself

It can be tremendous fun; it can also be painful when things don't go the way you want them to – and it's at these times that it can be very easy to give up. What is key to maintaining momentum and motivation around dating is to use it as an opportunity to practise being yourself. Give yourself permission to try things out, make mistakes, have successes, find out what you like and don't like and learn and grow from all your experiences. If you take this approach, it's much easier to avoid getting caught up in the emotion around dating that is usually related to our fear of rejection.

You're not going to find co... person you meet for a date, so, from the go of expectation. That way you'll reduce the disappointed and increase your resilience in the inevit... downs. The more people you see, the easier it becomes; and more people you see, the better your chances of meeting someone who is right for you.

Be the chooser

Dating is not just a great opportunity to practise what you have learned about yourself, it also gives you the chance to gain clarity about what it is you are seeking in a partner, so that when you do meet the person of your dreams, not only will your heart be speaking to you that this is the right one, but your head will know that you have found someone who matches your essential requirements and your core values at the very least.

When you meet someone who meets your criteria in this way, then you will know that the odds are stacked heavily in favour of this being a person with whom you could live out the vision of your ideal life. This whole book is about you being the chooser in life and in love. So many people fall into relationships because 'he or she was around and it seemed easy and I didn't want to be on my own'. Even if that has been your pattern before, it need never happen again.

If you were an organization wanting to fill a particular vacancy, you would be screening for certain essential, important and desirable criteria before you interviewed anyone. We advocated doing something similar in the last chapter when it came to deciding what you were seeking in a potential partner. Once you start to date, we strongly recommend that you meet several people to begin with so that you have a chance to screen them against your own criteria. You might find your requirements change slightly in the process.

Having a maximum of five requirements that you classify as essential does make the initial screening process much easier. If the person you are dating does not meet even one of these essential criteria and you choose to ignore this, then either it's not an essential requirement and you have it under the wrong heading or you are trying to turn a blind eye in the hope that the problem will go away. When you are consciously aware of what you are doing, then even ignoring the problem is a choice you make.

Stop trying and start wondering

In her book *Embracing Uncertainty* Susan Jeffers talks about the importance of having a sense of wonder about how our lives may unfold and how we can minimize disappointment by letting go of hope and expectation. Living in a 'wondering world' opens us up to possibility and takes away pressure about the future.

We would encourage you to move away from 'I have to find a partner by next year' or 'I hope I meet my soulmate within the next six months' to something more along the lines of, 'I wonder what next year will bring me on the relationship front?' By all means, keep hold of the intention that you wish to be in a relationship, but let go of being attached to it as something that has to happen. When we become obsessed with making something happen we get anxious about it, and this can stop us creating what we want because our anxiety actually sends out messages of desperation that are unattractive.

Expectation tends to close us down, whereas wondering opens us up to possibility.

Do what it takes to visualize the relationship of your dreams, as described in the final exercise in chapter 5, and then let go of the expectation and trust that the Universe will provide you with just what you are looking for – or something even better – whenever the time is right.

In the meantime, enjoy! And don't expect your first date to be 'The One'. A friend of ours once said, 'If I had only known, in my 20s, that I was going to meet the man of my dreams when I was in my 30s, I could have enjoyed myself so much more in those early years after I first left home.' Whatever your age, be curious and have fun. It will make the whole experience of dating so much more relaxed.

EXERCISE: MAKING LOVING CONNECTIONS

Here's a powerful exercise that will prepare you to set out to have fun and make lots of loving connections:

- If you could let go of any expectation of meeting your ideal partner, and knew that you could bring fun and a loving connection into your life whenever you wanted it, what would change for you? Imagine you are watching yourself on a television screen. Who are you with? How many people are there? What are you seeing and hearing? What are you saying to yourself? How are you feeling?

- Now turn up the volume and make the colours brighter and, when you have done that, imagine yourself stepping forward and into the picture.

- Imagine yourself right inside that picture. How are you feeling about yourself now that you are in it? If you're not feeling fantastic, then you haven't created the right picture for yourself, so you might want to choose another one.

- When you're ready, step out of the picture and know that you can create that picture for yourself whenever you want to, in just the way you have done here – by imagining you are stepping inside your own television screen.

- If you could act as if you already had as much fun and love in your life as you needed, what difference could that make to your life right now?

Where do you meet potential partners?

Well, as we've said earlier, you are not going to meet them by staying at home. So, it's important to put yourself in environments that will attract the sort of people you want to meet.

The more you share similar interests or values with the people you meet, the more likely it is that one of them will be right for you. Yes, you could meet someone in the supermarket and try to judge by his or her shopping trolley whether or not you have anything in common, but it might be hard to tell whether there is anything else you share other than a love of lettuce or southern fried chicken.

Chance encounters do happen and they do occasionally work, but the odds are not heavily stacked in their favour because you know nothing about each other beyond outer appearances. If you were advertising a job, would you take someone on just because they looked or sounded good? Wouldn't you want to know a bit more about them first? If you're looking for a partner, then for a start, how do you know if they are even available for a relationship?

These days there are a lot of organized singles events, including speed dating, slow dating, dinner dates and singles balls. These can be fun; they won't suit everyone, but if you feel like trying them, then go for it. Go with an open mind and without too much expectation, so that you don't get disappointed. If you set out with the intention of learning and having fun, then that is what will happen.

The only thing you usually know about the people who are attending a singles event is that they are single – which is a good start. Speed dating is, as its name implies, very speedy. Probably the best you can hope for in three minutes is to get an idea of who you are not attracted to. If you have both marked each other's card, the organizers will put you in touch with one another after the event and you can then find out whether or not you suit each other.

In the end, you may come away from many of these events feeling a bit disillusioned if you never seem to meet the right person – but don't forget that this is about practice. Finding out what you don't want is the first step to understanding what it is you actually do want. And you're getting the chance to try out flirting!

Improving the odds

If you are seriously looking for someone who is not only single, but who is going to meet your essential requirements for a long-term committed relationship, you need to think about putting yourself in environments where you will meet just that sort of person.

If you work in a large organization then you are lucky, because over 50 per cent of people who are in long-term relationships meet at work. If you don't, you will need to get creative.

Introduction agencies, dating agencies and internet dating, among others, all offer you the opportunity of seeking out specific types of people, and are safe ways of meeting new people provided you are sensible and arrange at least the first date in a public place. In fact, Ariana's agency, Real Connection, offers an exclusive introduction service for men to meet their life partners, but the guidelines are the same: proceed with caution. A combination of one or two emails and phone calls will soon tell you whether or not there is some hope of the two of you getting on but, sooner or later (and preferably sooner) you need to meet. No matter how well you have been able to communicate with each other beforehand, there is still an important part of the picture missing and until you meet you just won't know to what extent that part of the picture is a crucial factor.

Some dos and don'ts on internet dating

- A picture paints a thousand words, so make sure that you add yours. You will have a far greater response to your actual profile than to a profile statement.

- Have patience and enjoy the journey. Although it would be wonderful to meet the love of your life on the first or second date, it doesn't normally happen. Allow yourself time. If the fun goes out of it, stop immediately.

- Get very familiar with what you're looking for in a partner, and keep updating your own profile statement. Every time you update it, you go to the top of the list of searches.

- Create a reply template to everyone who sends you an email, and a simple 'thanks but no thanks message' that you can send out repeatedly if you don't want to pursue contact.

- Work out a standard response to a profile that does interest you. It might go 'I saw your profile and was interested in… You sound… and I'm interested in getting to know you better. If you are interested, please contact me.'

- After the initial email contact, arrange to speak to each other on the phone. In the interest of safety, it is normally advisable for the woman to phone the man and to bar her number before calling.

- Don't allow yourself to get too intimate on the phone. You might have a completely different view of the person once you meet!

- Beware the voice. Neither be put off at this early stage nor allow yourself to be seduced by mellifluous tones. Rarely does a voice match the person once you actually meet.

- Arrange the first couple of meetings in a public place and make sure that you let a friend know what you are doing.

- Keep the first date short. It's a good idea only to meet for a coffee on the first date. That gives you just enough time to check out whether you have enough in common and whether you want to take this further.

- The three-date rule: if your 'match' seems to meet your essential requirements but you don't feel the physical chemistry on the first date, don't begin to rule them out until you've had two to three dates. Chemistry can take time to develop.

- If you meet up and decide you don't want to go further, either tell your date at the end of the meeting or, if that feels too difficult, thank them at the end of the date and email them the next day. Treat people as you'd like to be treated yourself, everyone deserves to be respected.

- Use internet dating services as just one of several ways to meet people. Don't rely on this as the only source of possibility.

- Don't take it personally if someone does not follow up with you. It's usually nothing to do with you. If it happens and you are feeling hurt or disappointed, think of three alternative reasons why this could be (e.g. they realize they are not over a previous partner or you remind them of someone they don't like).

- Get a life and don't let internet dating take over yours. Internet dating can be overwhelming and time-consuming, and it certainly does not suit everyone. Remember that introduction agencies expect to come up with only about eight matches a year for each client. Be discriminating, and aim to meet up with no more than one person per week at the very most.

Developing your social circle

If agencies and the internet don't appeal to you, then you have to be even more creative about ways to meet people. Even if they do, we strongly advise you not to rely exclusively on them.

It is much better to expand your own life. Being able to choose to live your life exactly how you want is all part of being single and a free agent. Many people in relationships are envious of what they perceive to be the single person's freedom from compromise on how they live their life. However, if you're single, you know only too well that the single life has its ups and downs too. But you will also know by now that being in a relationship is not the be-all and end-all, as if you compromise too much you end up losing your own integrity.

Being single means you have the glorious opportunity to develop your own social circle of friends who fit in with your interests. As you do so, and as you get to know more people over a period of time, friendships with both sexes will develop. One of the best ways that we know of embarking on a relationship is when you have been friends first and chemistry has had time to grow.

Here are some ideas of things you could do and places you could go which would give you a chance to meet up with people who may share similar values and lifestyle to yours. Similar values and lifestyle are very important when you are looking for a soulmate, as the more you have in common to start with, the better. You are bound to think of other types of meeting places. And give yourself time to get to know people. Don't dismiss them out of hand because you see no partner potential. Remember, you're out to have fun first and foremost.

- sporting clubs
- wine tastings
- singing groups
- personal growth workshops
- special interest talks
- art classes
- religious/spiritual groups

- volunteer organizations
- committee work
- evening classes
- live music clubs
- business network meetings
- foreign language classes
- dancing
- travel/adventure clubs

You know how easy it is to have good intentions about expanding your network and then doing absolutely nothing about it.

> *If you always do what you've always done, you'll always get what you've always got.*
>
> Anon.

Now is your chance to do something different.

EXERCISE: DEVELOPING A SOCIAL CIRCLE

Get your pen out and start thinking about how you can start to develop a social circle of your own.

- Think of some hobbies or interests that you would love to pursue but that are outside the comfort zone of your existing social circle. If you are actively seeking a partner, then make sure these are activities where you will meet people of the appropriate sex. If you can't think of anything, then brainstorm up to 10 ideas with a friend or with your coach.
- Choose one idea and find out where and how you could do it. And here's an important question: what would stop you from doing it? Be aware in advance of how you might sabotage yourself. It's no good saying you haven't got time, because if you haven't got time to pursue an interest, then you certainly haven't got time for a relationship.

- If you are feeling some resistance, then break the activity down into small steps, e.g. (1) research jazz clubs, (2) find a friend to go with, (3) agree when you are going to go, (4) then do it.

- Then commit to doing it for a month or two. If that doesn't work for you, look at your list again and try something else. But don't give up after the first attempt, and certainly don't give up if you enjoy the activity even if there don't, at first, appear to be any potential love partners. You need to give these things time.

Projection and fantasy

We don't see things as they are, we see things as we are.
Anaïs Nin, writer (1903–77)

A chapter on dating would not be complete without a look at some of the underlying psychological processes that go on when we first meet someone. Even simply reading a profile on the internet or talking on the telephone can be enough for us to start fantasizing or projecting our own desires on to someone.

Projection: seeing what you want

We do this with people when we talk to them and when we meet. There maybe something about the way they hold their head or look at us that results in our 'seeing' a quality in them that is actually something we want in ourselves or find it hard to acknowledge that we already have. And so we project that quality onto them; a bit like a projector throwing the image of the celluloid film onto a screen, only in this case other people are our screens.

You are not alone in doing this, it's something we all do. 'Projection' actually means 'attributing one's unconscious desires [those that are hidden even from ourselves] on to someone else'. We do it in particular with certain people, especially new omantic partners.

At first you seem to have so much in common: you share a similar sense of humour and you fancy each other hugely. You really want that person to be right for you, and so you find every way you can to fit them into your perfect mould, which is not really their mould at all; rather, it's how you want them to be.

As a marriage guidance counsellor, Ariana often asked couples what it was about each other that they were attracted to in the early stages of their relationship. Often, what had brought them to the counselling room was the discovery that their projections were wrong, which left them feeling let down and angry. Jim might have thought Susan was fun and exciting to be with when he first met her but, ten years on, he resents her for being too much of a social butterfly and never wanting to be at home to put a meal on the table for him. By the same token, Susan loved the feeling of stability that Jim gave her when they first met. He was calm and sensible and created a perfect foil for her passionate nature. Now, however, she resents him for being boring and unsociable. Each of them feels justified in their scorn of the other. And yet neither of them has really changed.

Andrea's Story

When Andrea first met her husband, she heard him talking on the phone to one of his clients. She liked the way he spoke with what she perceived as authority and knowledge; she felt she was with someone who knew what he was doing and could communicate clearly. This fulfilled her need for a sense of security. If he was so knowledgable and could sort out all his client's problems then he'd be able to look after her!

What Andrea was actually doing was projecting her need for security on to her future husband, and the hook for this was his voice and manner. She was attributing to him knowledge and authority and denying that she had these qualities herself. She was also wanting him to provide her with security rather than developing her own strong personal foundation.

As the relationship developed, the projections receded and Andrea began to see her husband in his true light. It turned out he was no more secure than she was financially, and that he was very insecure in himself, too. He used his authoritative manner, which she'd originally perceived so positively, to try to control her and put her down in a 'You're not OK' position. This led to dreadful arguments and fights; Andrea lost her sense of self-esteem and became a shadow of her former self. She eventually found the resources to leave the marriage.

On reflecting why things had gone so wrong for her in this relationship, Andrea realized how much responsibility for herself she'd given up on the basis of the projections she'd placed on her husband. After her marriage was over she chose to work on building up her own sense of self-love and security before she entered another relationship.

If you find yourself pinning your hopes and dreams on what you see in another person, then you are most definitely projecting something on to them and it's worth asking yourself:

- What is it about the type of people I'm attracted to that I am not recognizing within myself?

   And also:

- How might I be attributing qualities to my potential partner so that I can avoid taking responsibility for myself?

As we said earlier, projection is something we all do, so how do we deal with our own projections? The first step is to recognize that this is what you are doing and to admit honestly what you might not be facing up to in yourself. Sharing your experiences with friends is also a useful way to check whether you're viewing someone in an overly positive or negative light. If you are able to talk freely with the person you are dating, you could even check with them how real your projection is.

If Andrea had asked her husband-to-be a few more pertinent questions she would have got a very different picture from the one she imagined (more of this in chapter 7). We cannot make our projections disappear completely , but with awareness we can at least make choices based on the whole picture.

Fantasy: making up the story

How many of us have succeeded in making up a whole story about the life we might live with a person we don't even know very well?

This is called 'fantasy', and is different from projection because we build up a whole fictional scenario in our mind. We often do this when we are very much in need and want a quick escape from the discomfort of our present; hence the importance of getting our needs met and living a happy, fulfilled life before seeking a partner.

As with projection, we usually 'fantasize' unconsciously. Our dream may be about getting someone else to take responsibility for us, to rescue us or bail us out and to provide us with the fulfilled relationship we've never experienced consistently before. We then create a 'fantasy' around how we might get them to do that.

ARIANA'S STORY: When an email came through via one internet dating site from a man who seemed, on the face of it, to meet all my requirements and to be in touch with his feminine side, I decided he was someone I wanted to reply to.

His next email seemed to offer too good an opportunity to miss:

'I am a loving, attractive, fun, kind, intelligent, interesting, well-travelled, passionate, generous, successful guy with a huge zest for life, and many interests that match yours. I have a place in London, an apartment at Villars in the Swiss mountains next to the ski lift, a floating home of 60-foot in length, and a very warm heart and soul, which is the ultimate place of all!'

This man was wealthy, an added bonus that I had not anticipated – and in a flash I had planned my future with him! If anyone ought to know better, I should. But I was hooked. How could a girl resist? Here was somebody who seemed to share my values and my passions, and was financially more than able to keep me in comfort. I even paced out 60 feet and decided that was big enough for me. A flat in Villars; I could just picture myself coaching from there, as most of my work is done by phone, and running small cozy work-shops on the yacht – I had it all worked out and I hadn't even spoken to him.

Well, no doubt you've guessed, despite numerous emails between us, he didn't actually call. Goodness knows where this guy was coming from and it really doesn't matter. The point is that all my old insecurities around money and self-worth had come to a head and, although I knew they were there, I had still managed to concoct a wild fantasy about something that I secretly hoped for: someone to rescue me and keep me in the manner to which I longed to become accustomed. This was a sure-fire way of putting me right back into a co-dependent relationship, just like the one I had come out of in my marriage only the year before.

I knew that what I really needed was to prove to myself that I could stand on my own two feet, so that I could eventually be in a relationship with someone on an equal footing rather than, as I had felt in my marriage, always slightly out of control. But I realized that my old rescue fantasy could hook me in and pull me right back to where I started, and this experience was a useful reminder of how important it was that I took responsibility for getting one of my most important needs met before seeking a relationship.

The 'if only' trap

This is a variation on the projection theme. 'I've just met the man of my dreams. He would be perfect, if only he didn't drink so heavily. I want to do what I can for him because he has been beset by bad luck throughout most of his life. If I can just show him how much I love him and help him to get some counselling about his drinking, he will surely change.'

Or: 'I've just met my ideal woman. She is everything I ever wanted. If only she didn't go shopping so much. But I know I can help her to become more responsible and she will surely change.'

These people are seeing perfection where it doesn't exist and minimizing the importance of the problem between them. They think they can 'fix' the other person. The reason for this is that they are seeking to get their needs met by the other person and that, in turn, causes them to ignore the truth about the relationship and how it will be in the future. The real test of whether someone is right for you is: 'Can you be with them just as they are right now, without them ever changing?'

It is far better to choose people whom you can love without trying to change them. And it is amazing how many clues we get about someone in the early stages of a relationship or before it has even begun if we have strengthened our personal foundation enough to understand which of our needs drive us. If we take responsibility for getting these needs met ourselves, then we are less likely to fall for people for the wrong reasons.

No one can persuade another to change. Each of us guards a gate
of change that can only be opened from the inside. We cannot
open the gate of another, either by argument or emotional appeal.

Marilyn Ferguson (b.1938)

EXERCISE: HOW DO YOU PROJECT?

- What needs are you expecting prospective partners to meet for you (look back at the work you did on this in chapter 5)?
- What fantasies have you projected onto past relationships that have idealized them for you?
- What potential problems about these relationships did you choose to turn a blind eye to?
- What has been the truth in the end?

Maintaining your motivation for dating

Dating can be tremendous fun, it can also be an energy drain if we allow it to be. We have already noted certain things in this chapter that you can do to keep your motivation strong, to enable you to enjoy meeting new people, to avoid expectation and cultivate a 'wondering' approach. Use the opportunity to practise being the real you and to listen, to observe without judging and to ask for your needs to be met.

Here are a few more ideas to keep you tuned in to the fun of dating.

- Do things and go to places you've always really wanted to visit. Think about all the things you've wondered about doing and haven't done for ages: maybe drinks at the Ritz, meeting at a well-known restaurant or visiting an art exhibition that interests you. Make sure the venue is somewhere you can both talk, but where there is an alternative motivation other than meeting your date. That way you're combining two experiences in one – and if the date doesn't come off, then at least you've seen some paintings that interested you or had a drink or meal in great surroundings!

- Be discerning about whom you meet. This applies particularly to people you meet over the internet. It can be very demoralizing to meet people and find you have hardly anything in common; if this keeps happening to you, then make sure you check your potential dates out more carefully before meeting. You can tell a lot by how you relate to someone on the telephone and/or email.
- Does your contact dominate the conversations and spend the time talking only about themselves?
- Does your contact ask you anything about yourself?
- Is it easy to talk and relate to each other over the phone?
- Do you appear to have enough in common to make meeting up worthwhile?

Your answers to these questions will help you decide whether you want to go ahead and meet your contact or not.

- Create a network of dating buddies. If you are the only one of your friends who is dating then it can be very hard to maintain your energy and excitement about it. If you link up with contacts and friends who are also out there meeting people, you can support each other when things don't go as you'd have liked them to, and also share the fun and laughter of your good experiences.

Have fun and get flirty

Why is it that some people are just natural flirts and people magnets? We all know someone like that, and stand in awe as we watch members of the opposite sex just naturally gravitate in their direction. How do they do it?

Flirting is all about having fun, being in the moment and being yourself. So shouldn't we all be trying to flirt with life a little more – catching people's eyes, laughing and smiling, and generally allowing ourselves not to get quite so hung up about how we come across, and instead focusing more on what's going on with those around us?

If you start practising being authentic with as many people as possible, you'll begin to realize how similar this is to flirting; people will respond to you but in a much more open and honest way. Be curious and interested in other people and remember that everyone has unique qualities that make them who they are. Look for those qualities and pay attention to them. This is an irresistibly attractive approach. If you try to be what you are not, then at some point you are going to get found out.

And just to help you along the way, here are some ideas you can practise.

- *Practise flirting with life.* Catch people's eyes and say 'Hi' or 'Good morning' or 'Lovely today, isn't it?' As Peta Heskell from the Attraction Academy says: 'If you see someone without a smile, give them one of yours.'

- *What makes you unique and wonderful?* Ask your friends. Create a treasure box and, every time you receive a gift or a compliment that reminds you how much you are appreciated for being the wonderful person you are, pop it in there. Then, whenever you are feeling a bit down, get the box out and give yourself a reminder.

- *Celebrate your uniqueness* by concentrating on what's great about you, rather than focusing on what you're no good at. Write some positive affirmations on index cards and repeat them throughout the day, every day for at least 21 days, so it becomes a habit.

- *Get into your body.* Notice your body when you are feeling confident. The way that you hold yourself, your body movements, facial expressions and eye contact all send out signals about how you are feeling. Even if you are not feeling confident, pretend to your body that you are. Tell yourself that you are, and notice how your body responds to the messages you give yourself.

- *Don't compare yourself with other people.* There will always be someone who is cleverer, prettier, more handsome, more articulate and more skilled than you are. So choose not to focus on that but to focus on what is good about you instead.

- *'Walk in another man's moccasins'* and learn to see the world from other people's perspectives. If you can do this, you will start flexing your rapport muscles, honing your ability to connect deeply with others. It is a powerful technique and will help you to stop feeling self-conscious because you will be concentrating on the other person more than on yourself.

- *Be curious.* People love it if you show genuine interest in them, so get used to asking questions starting with words such as who, what, where, when and how – and be prepared to share information about yourself, too.

- *If you're nervous,* take a deep breath as you count to 6. Hold it for 6 then breathe out to a count of 12. Do it again, then feel the fear and go for it. What's the worst thing that could happen anyway? People who are brave still feel the fear, they just choose to take their fear with them.

- *Concentrate on loving yourself* and on making your own life as magical as possible – and then notice how opportunities (and dates) start to come your way.

Maintaining momentum after being rejected

We all carry a fear of not being liked or loved and of being rejected. Yet rejection is something you are likely to have to face at some point, simply by being out there and dating people. All of us will have experienced it at one time or another. Rejection while dating can be a blow to your confidence and it can make you want to run back into the shadows of your cozy and safe comfort zone and hide under the duvet.

This is where having a support network is really important, so that you don't have to deal with this on your own. Get on the phone to a really close friend and get it off your chest. Have a moan, a whinge and a weep if that helps you to get it out of your system – but don't let one or two rejections stop you from holding out for what you want. Maybe you thought you had met 'the one'; but there are plenty of 'ones' out there, and if you retreat you are giving up your power and you certainly won't meet them.

If you are really distressed by a particular rejection, then consider what is it about this person that has hooked you. Imagine you are in a helicopter looking down at you from a distance, enabling you to get a clearer perspective. What have you projected onto this person, what fantasy have you constructed that is making them seem so perfect, and how is this preventing you from seeing that person as a whole being with both good and bad bits?

Carry on dating. But if you do need time to lick your wounds and recover, then by all means give yourself a break. Just take care not to withdraw so far that you make it really hard for yourself to get going again. Who knows what is waiting for you just round the corner? Use every experience you have to keep learning and to become stronger about yourself and knowing what it is you want.

Whether – and when – to have sex

And, for that matter, that first kiss…

It's easy to say, just do what feels right, but lust can so easily distort one's perceptions and judgement, and you don't want to have to extricate yourself from a situation that has gone horribly wrong.

M. Scott Peck's book *The Road Less Travelled* is concerned with spiritual rather than physical themes; nonetheless he talks about 'delaying gratification' and that seems to be a good rule of thumb here, too.

Setting boundaries

Remember that you are in control of yourself; you have the power to be the chooser. You don't have to have to go out with anyone just because you feel grateful to have been chosen, nor do you have to kiss them or have sex with them unless you feel ready to do so. Even when you feel ready to do so, you have the power to choose whether it is right at that moment or whether delaying gratification might be more prudent.

There are no hard and fast rules. We can only suggest that on your first date, you limit kissing to a peck on the cheek or lips only. Give yourself time to get to know someone before the kisses become more lingering. Set your own guidelines to when you feel comfortable about getting into kissing and caressing, although we suggest you don't get into heavy petting until you have decided you want to go on seeing someone. It is fine to be flirtatious and sexy, so long as you don't over-tease.

You will make life far less complicated for yourself if you really get to know your partner and decide whether you are intellectually and emotionally compatible before you sleep together. We talk more about this in the next chapter on the testing phase and the dangers of the 'mini-marriage'. If you are thinking of having sex with your new love, read this now.

Think about your essential requirements. Are they being met by this person? Do you really like them? Do you share their values or are you just sexually attracted to them? Be clear why you want to have a sexual relationship with them, because once you do you put the relationship on a whole different level. Unless you want the same things from the relationship, one of you could get hurt. And, above all, use the necessary precautions to avoid sexually transmitted diseases and pregnancy; otherwise don't do it.

Decide now what boundaries you wish to set for yourself around sexual intimacy.

Jane and Martin's Story

Jane and Martin had been introduced at a party, and since then had seen each other several times. They enjoyed each other's company and shared a lot in common. However, he had been honest with her and had told her that he was having a long-distance sexual relationship with someone called Deborah.

He had been talking about ending the relationship with Deborah. She was very involved with her career and they weren't able to see each other very often. The relationship seemed to be going nowhere although, just before Jane and Martin had first met, he and Deborah had recently spent a few days together in the south of France.

Jane realized that it was early days, but she knew that Martin was someone she could imagine having a long-term committed relationship with. They had a lot in common and were both sexually attracted to one another. However, the boundaries that Jane had set for herself were very clear and she knew that if she ignored her own guidelines then she would be compromising her emotional security at her peril.

Martin knew that he and Deborah did not have a long-term future and that he was seeking a more committed relationship. He realized it was not fair to keep all his options open and really didn't want to lose Jane, whom he respected. He and his former girlfriend parted amicably and he started a relationship with Jane, who was glad she had been so clear about what was important to her.

If you are dating other people you might want to consider becoming exclusive as a couple before you have sex. Internet dating provides a useful metaphor for this in that many couples will suspend their profiles before moving into the more sexually intimate stage of sleeping together. It is so much easier to set boundaries around these sorts of issues before having sex; it's much more difficult to do it afterwards.

Of course, you can set your boundaries however you like and rules are sometimes meant to be broken. But it is worth taking some time to think about this issue so that you are clear what it is you want when you first start seeing someone and before you get sexually involved.

Sexual chemistry

If you hadn't gathered by now, love is blind.

Now, that might not be something you want to hear. After all, you've been in love. You know what it feels like. Heart pounding. Breathlessness. Sleeplessness. Loss of appetite. 'If the world has to come to an end, please God, at least make sure we die together.' 'Nobody else in the whole world has ever felt like this.'

And yet... of course, so often the dream does die. At the very least, if you have ever experienced any of the feelings mentioned in the last paragraph you will know that they do change. You would be exhausted if you felt that way all the time. It would be like taking amphetamines permanently – at some point you have to come off them.

Some people, however, addicted to the high that falling in lust (because that is what it really is) gives them, remain on a permanent roller-coaster, mistaking lust for love and becoming disillusioned when they fall out of lust and begin to see their partner as just a mere human after all. Often they have chosen a partner who is totally unsuitable for them anyway, but they just can't see it at first, so blinded are they by their all-consuming passion. And when that relationship fails they go on to seek the same experience with someone else. And so their life roller-coasts along in a series of extreme highs and lows, an endlessly search for a relationship filled with never-ending passion.

Short-term sexual chemistry tends to distort reality and can cause us to ignore warning signals. Initially, sexual attraction releases an adrenaline-like substance called phenylethylamine (PEA), together with neurochemicals known as dopamine and norephinephrine, which are natural mood enhancers similar to amphetamines. And so your heart beats faster and fantasies can go into overdrive. This feeling can last anything from six months to two years.

After orgasm we produce an endorphin called oxytocin, which provides a sense of calm and safety, and causes people to feel peaceful, loving and secure. Oxytocin also exists in a good long-term relationship, and remains long after the addictive PEA and neurochemicals have disappeared.

Be careful not to mistake lust for love, and beware making any decisions about your long-term future with a partner while you are still in those heady early days. Although 'love at first sight' seems like a wonderful concept, and you may think you know when you have met someone with whom you will spend the rest of your life, unfortunately the divorce statistics (which include our own) prove otherwise.

Inclusive versus exclusive relationships

It is also worth giving some thought to the type of relationship you are seeking at this point, as that may also inform your decision on sexual involvement. After working through chapters 4 and 5, you may have decided that you are not yet ready for a committed relationship. Maybe you still have some work to do on getting some of the other areas of your life into balance, or maybe you are still getting over your last relationship and don't feel ready to get emotionally involved just yet.

But you miss having male or female company and you have decided that you want to go out and have some fun. In America, it is perfectly normal to date several people at the same time. It is far less common in the UK, although there is no reason why it should be. We suggest that if you simply want to date and have fun, but do not want to have an exclusive relationship with one person, you communicate this clearly to your date. You may find that they feel exactly the same way, and you will have taken the pressure out of the situation. If they don't, then it's better for you both to know sooner, rather than later. Knowledge allows you both to make informed choices.

EXERCISE: SETTING YOUR OWN GUIDELINES

Decide the following:

- Are you seeking a long-term committed relationship or are you just looking to have some dating experience and fun?
- What personal guidelines do you intend to set yourself around sexual intimacy with a new partner?

Practice does make perfect, so give yourself permission to do loads of practising. There are a lot of single people out there, of all different ages and types, all seeking their ideal mate. And after all, you only need to find one!

> *All my experiences are opportunities to gain more power, clarity and vision.*
>
> Sanaya Roman and Duane Packer, authors of *Creating Money: Keys to Abundance*

7

Testing the Waters

> *I'm not willing to gamble my whole life on someone who is not quite sure. I'm still looking for something more extraordinary than that.*

From *Bridget Jones's Diary* by Helen Fielding (b.1960)

To develop a long-term relationship or life partnership, you will need to give each other and your relationship *real* quality time together so that you *really* get to know each other. This will give you the chance to check out how well you and your partner meet each other's requirements. It's important to do this before fully committing, when it's easier to stop the relationship, should you discover things don't match up.

We hope that by the end of this chapter you will have:
- learned how to make a conscious evaluation of a new relationship by balancing your head and your heart;
- gained insight into how entering into a mini-marriage could lead to a mini-divorce;
- learned some ways to test for your requirements and make sure that these are met;
- learned how to use this phase as an opportunity to get to know your partner properly before making a commitment;
- become clearer about when is a good time to begin a sexual relationship with a new partner;
- developed some skills and insight on how to end a relationship respectfully if you find it's not the one for you.

Into the honeymoon phase

In our exploration of relationships we're now moving beyond dating and into the honeymoon phase. The chemistry is at work as we connect and get to know each other, share new experiences together and start to learn about each other; this phase is extremely exciting, and can be characterized by a sense that our experiences and feelings have almost merged.

You may well have been seeing more than one person while you were dating, but this chapter looks at what happens when you have met someone with whom you want to have a more serious relationship, one that excludes dating other people. You are now ready for the testing phase.

A note about exclusivity and commitment

Sometimes people muddle up exclusivity with commitment, so let's see how the two differ. Exclusivity is about having only one partner. Whereas commitment is about stepping forward and agreeing that you are going to be long-term partners who will share and willingly work through joys and challenges together. Many people choose marriage at this point.

Exclusivity is usually part of a committed relationship, but you can be in an exclusive relationship and know that you are not ready to commit. Testing out how well a relationship works for you, therefore, is something that takes place within the boundaries of an exclusive relationship and needs to come before you make any sort of long-term commitment.

Beware the mini-marriage

Many people in the early stages of a relationship enter into a kind of 'mini-marriage' without having tested out the relationship first. They may move in together; they may even have a child. Sadly, when the intensity of the chemistry wears off or problems arise in the relationship, and the couple find they are incompatible or unable to communicate well together, the end result is often a 'mini-divorce', which can be heartbreaking and stressful for all concerned.

You may have experienced this yourself and have despaired of ever finding a fulfilling relationship that does not lead to heartache in the end. It doesn't have to be like that if you take the time to get to know your partner really well and test out the relationship before becoming committed.

If you don't like the sound of this...

Perhaps the last thing you want to do is start getting logical and checking out whether your new partner is right for you or not when it's all so new and exciting.

However, while in the short term you might be having a great time, consider the long-term consequences of not testing things out in your new relationship.

Take a look at what happened with Alana and Jed.

Alana and Jed's Story

Alana met Jed when she was in her mid-30s, after a fairly long period of being single. She was keen to be in a long-term relationship again. Most of her friends had settled down; she also knew she wanted to have children, and her biological clock was ticking.

Alana wasn't that sure about Jed when she first met him. He was very different from anyone she'd been out with before. He was much quieter, a real softy, the perfect gentlemen and a lot older than her. However, she thought she'd give it a go and he very quickly made it clear he liked her a lot. This really boosted Alana's ego and she started having a great time with him. They spoke every day on the phone; slept together on the third date – and of course the sex was great – the best she'd ever had! By the end of the month they were absolutely committed to each other and 'in love'. Jed gave Alana the kind of devoted attention she'd been craving and she was the warm, creative and intelligent woman he'd been looking for. They quickly got engaged and set a date for the wedding.

During this period there were two or three times when Alana saw a side to Jed she felt uncomfortable about. He lost his temper with other people

*for what seemed no good reason, shouting and swearing at them. Yet
Alana put her discomfort to the back of her mind. She wanted a husband
and Jed was always absolutely respectful, kind and loving to her. They went
ahead and married.*

*Within months, the devotion Jed had showered on Alana in the early
days turned to critical comments and she began to wonder what on
earth she'd done. It seemed she could never do anything right. She had
imagined their weekends would be spent sharing activities they both
enjoyed – going for walks, visiting friends or entertaining, going to the
theatre or galleries. In reality, Jed either wanted to stay at home and watch
television or go to a football match. And he resented her friends coming
round. They both realized they had very little in common. At the time they
married, they had thought they were in love and that each was the other's
ideal mate. The reality was a different story.*

Making time for testing

No matter what life stage you are at, if you are looking for long-term
relationship happiness there is real merit in investing time in the
early honeymoon phase, taking things at a reasonable pace and
building a strong foundation together on which both of you and the
relationship can thrive.

It's odd, really. We know people who spend weeks looking for and
checking out the specifications of a new sofa, computer or car, yet
when it comes to a new relationship they are prepared to throw
themselves in without doing any research.

Research by child psychiatrist John Bowlby found that children
who have disrupted childhoods, where they are separated from
their mothers in the first three years or are taken into care, are much
more likely to be indiscriminate in whom they go to for affection
and care. Early experiences of love and intimacy profoundly affect
how we make relationships as adults, and even those of us who
have had consistently loving experiences as children will still be
influenced by those experiences in how we mate and relate.

The more quickly a person falls 'in love' and becomes attached to
someone, the greater the likelihood that there are issues in their life
around love and intimacy that have not been addressed. Remember

we talked about co-dependency in chapter 5? Old, painful experiences create gaps in ourselves that we want our partner or our relationship to fill.

Beware of that trap. Ensure that what is happening between you and your partner is the creation of a genuinely loving and respectful relationship, where each of you can be yourself and where neither of you feels you are giving up on yourself. True knowledge, beyond initial chemistry, takes time; and it is only time that will tell whether or not you are compatible. Yes, there are exceptions; but on the whole, the more quickly you become intimate, the more likely it is that the relationship is built on chemistry – which, as you know by now, will change – rather than true compatibility.

Alana and Jed's situation is not uncommon. Many people launch into a relationship without ever really thinking about whether their new partner is right for them, let alone testing this out. This can result in enormous emotional, physical and financial costs to both parties, as in Alana and Jed's case when they eventually did part.

So you can see why we place so much emphasis on testing during the honeymoon phase *before* you make a commitment.

Love and 'in love'

This is an appropriate place to give some attention to that magical and all-important word 'love'. We strongly believe that where love exists the world is most certainly a better place.

But what is love? Well, first of all, it's a feeling: 'I love you so much'. It's also a thought and an intention: 'I want to give love to you'.

Love takes many forms. The love a parent feels for a child is different from the love between friends, and this is different again from the love between two people in an intimate relationship.

Loving someone is different from being in love with them. When you love someone, you may care for them, give to them, cherish and adore them, but you hold on to a sense of your own self as well and know that it's important to take care of yourself, too.

Being 'in love' is like falling under a spell. We become irrational, we go out of our way to do anything we can for the other person, even to the extent of abandoning our own needs. As we have just seen, relationship psychologists say that when we fall 'in love' we are often experiencing unresolved feelings and needs left over from early childhood, needs that we are hoping our partner will meet. Of course, we're not aware that we are doing this; but the stronger and more intense the feeling, the more it indicates unfinished business that will interfere with our ability to develop the sort of inter-dependent relationship we discussed in chapter 5.

In *The Seven Habits of Highly Effective People* Steven Covey talks about 'love' being an action verb; it is something we need to keep practising, rather than focusing on being. When we *do* loving things, such as listening to our partner, taking time to notice how special they are, making gestures that nurture and strengthen the relationship, we are in a far more empowered position. By contrast, if we surrender to love as just being a feeling, then we are in effect giving up our power: 'I can't help it, I love him/her so much.'

So, ask yourself now:
- How often do you give up on yourself?
- Are you prepared to put up with unacceptable behaviour because you are 'in love'?

Entertain and hold the notion for yourself that loving someone is a far healthier and happier thing to be doing than being 'in love' with someone.

How do you go about testing?

In chapter 5 you created lists of essential, important and desirable requirements to help you focus on what it is you really want in a relationship. Well, now is the time to check how far your partner really does meet your specific requirements.

When we first date someone we fancy we often go out of our way to be agreeable and to find areas of common ground. Alana and Jed used to visit art galleries together when they first met, which was something she loved; yet once they were married they did not sustain that interest together. Alana appeared to be interested in football when she first met Jed; yet once the magic had worn off she was quite open about her lack of enthusiasm.

We may have a tendency to 'market' ourselves by adopting behaviour that we know will please our partner and win their approval of us. However, this behaviour is not necessarily true to ourselves, and as we become more intimate our partner may discover that we are not actually the person we seemed to be at all and vice versa.

Balancing head and heart

Having your essential criteria set out helps you to take a more objective approach at a time when it may be very hard to keep your head.

Here are a few further tips that will help you check your feelings and gauge how well your essential requirements are being met when you are in the early stages of a relationship.

- Share your requirements with a friend. Ask them to challenge you when you are in danger of losing your perspective and are prepared to ignore some of your essential criteria. Choose someone who will be straight with you.

- Keep a journal and really be honest with yourself. Make a note of any doubts that may come up that you may be trying to ignore. This is not about being disloyal to your new love; record the good stuff too, so that you have a balanced view.

- Keep asking yourself, what do I want from this relationship? Does this person have long-term potential? What am I turning a blind eye to now that could come back and haunt me in years to come? Who or what does this person represent for me?

ARIANA'S STORY: Having spent 20 years in two long-term relationships with partners who were supporting their children, I was very clear that I did not want a repeat run. I now wanted a long-term relationship where, finally, my needs would not come second.

However, clear as I was in my own mind about not wanting to get involved with anyone who was supporting young children, let alone an ex-wife, I found it incredibly hard to balance my heart with my head when I met someone with whom there was an obvious spark.

It helped to be reminded (usually by Mary) what my essential requirements were, and I know I surprised some men when, despite obvious chemistry between us, I would tell them quite clearly that a long-term relationship was out of the question because one of my essential requirements was not being met. Love, in my experience, did not always conquer all, and for me to ignore something that I had deemed to be non-negotiable was nothing less than foolhardy.

Being clear about my non-negotiable requirements helped me to keep my feet planted firmly on the ground and, although that might sound less than romantic, it meant that I was being the chooser in my life and in my future at long last.

Question, listen and observe

The exercise in this section sets out some useful themes and questions to help stimulate conversation with your partner so you can begin to put together a picture of how compatible you are.

As you ask the questions, listen and observe and try and avoid reacting immediately.

A friend of ours was definitely in lust with her new date, but her instinct was telling her that he was still getting over his previous relationship, which had lasted for five years and had broken up only three months before. She therefore prepared some questions she wanted to ask him about this.

When they began to discuss his past relationship, he immediately assured her he was totally over it and wanted to be with her. She decided to dump all her other questions, threw caution to the wind and committed herself to the relationship. A couple of months later she was devastated when he told her he couldn't continue in the relationship as he realized he wasn't ready to settle down.

Testing that your essential requirements are truly being met *before* you commit is very important to long-term well-being, so take your time and don't rush things. You have the rest of your life to be with that special someone if they are the right person for you. The old saying 'act in haste, repent at leisure' is never more true than when you commit yourself to a relationship that turns out to be the wrong one.

EXERCISE: OPENING UP LINES OF COMMUNICATION

Use the following themes and questions to help open up lines of communication with your partner. The only requirement is a mutual willingness to share thoughts and feelings, and to listen to each other with love, compassion and respect.

- Talk about one specific way in which you are different from most people of your sex. How has this affected you? How does it affect others?

- Describe something that makes you laugh and explain why.

- Discuss someone who has been a major influence in your life, for good or bad. Describe the ways this person has affected you.

- Talk about someone who broke your heart. Why did this happen? How did you react? What do you think you were meant to learn? What have you done to heal the pain from this relationship?

- Describe what you like and dislike most about the opposite sex.

- Describe something about yourself that even those closest to you have sometimes misunderstood.

- Discuss any religious or spiritual beliefs you had when you were growing up. How have your beliefs changed since then?

- Talk about what you are most proud of about yourself and why?

- Discuss whether you have ever seen your father or other male role model cry? How did this affect you? If you haven't experienced this, how do you think it would make you feel?

- Talk about a trait you particularly dislike in other people. Why does it bother you so much? Have you ever found this trait in yourself, too?

Source: CoupleConnect cards

Move from talking to doing

Having a clear note of how your essential requirements translate into behaviour enables you to check that your partner really does meet them in practice.

For example, if an 'adventurous spirit' is an important requirement, what does that actually mean for you? What would tell you that someone has got an adventurous spirit? Well, for a start, finding out if someone likes to travel and explore would give you an idea. But your partner might want to please you by saying they enjoy travelling and exploring (remember how we sometimes market ourselves). So, if it is really important for you to have a partner to share in these activities, then you may want to check this out by trying new experiences and seeing not only how you are together when you do this, but how your partner responds and reacts in these situations.

One couple we know both loved travel, but when they did so they discovered that he wanted to get right out of the touristy places and to experience ethnic culture, while she preferred the luxury of the top-notch hotels, restaurants and shops. Now, this may not be grounds for ending a relationship, but it will affect how you are together and does reflect very different values. The more difference there is between your respective values, the more you may find your interests are in conflict.

Observation is also important, as it moves you away from hearing the story to seeing the reality. Always keep an eye out for how someone reacts and behaves and how you feel in response to this. What would you think if someone were to say to you, 'Oh yes, looking after myself is really important,' and yet proceeded to smoke 20 cigarettes a day and never exercise? What if you met someone who said, 'I want a relationship where we are both equal', and yet did nothing around the house and expected you to organize everything? Are their actions matching their words?

What jars with you?

Even when we're feeling passionately in love with someone there can still be moments or times when things about them jar with us.

Some things can appear quite superficial and seem to have little meaning, but it is certainly worth making a mental note of your gut reactions in the early days, because they might indicate things that could build up into major irritants and causes of conflict later. For example, a perceived lack of dress sense might be just that; or it could indicate a lack of self-care.

Alana, whose story we looked at on page 150, had chosen to turn a blind eye to Jed's behaviour with other people, hoping he might change. In fact, things only got worse after they were married as he started to turn his temper on her.

Beware of building your hopes and dreams of relationship success on 'potential'. Thinking your relationship has potential is putting your focus on the future, rather than dealing with the present. You're on much more solid ground if you focus on what is happening now. If what's happening now is what you want, then this is a great indicator that you have a great relationship. If it isn't, then take note – you may be storing up trouble for yourself down the line.

Also be aware that all the positive things you are experiencing in the early stages of your relationship may cause you to avoid some of the more serious issues between you. It's understandable that you might not want to confront a tricky situation when things are going well between you. But when things are going well is precisely the best time to deal with anything that is not working properly. You may risk rejection – but how might you feel in six months' time, if you continue not to discuss the issue? Or you might manage to resolve the issue between you, which is indeed the purpose of the whole exercise.

If confrontation is something you find difficult and prefer to avoid, you may benefit from the additional discussion of communication in the next chapter. In the meantime, just take care that you are not putting a positive slant on something that is really not OK for you. Ask yourself this question, which we use in coaching: 'In saying yes to this, what am I saying no to?' Are you giving up on any dreams in order to be with this particular person? Are you compromising any of your values? Keep checking that your essential requirements are being met.

Keeping your journal is especially important at this time. You can note your doubts without analyzing them and just see if they keep being repeated. If they do, then this is telling you something is not working for you and needs to be addressed in some way.

Have a row!

We're not suggesting you orchestrate a row deliberately, but we are suggesting that you are in no position to decide if someone is right for you or not until you've found out how you both deal with conflict and difference. Some experts say that until you've had your first row you shouldn't even contemplate a long-term relationship.

Anger is part of life, and it's a way that we keep ourselves defined and separate. If I don't ever feel anger or frustration, then how do I know when something is happening that goes against my personal values or needs?

How we deal with anger is another thing, so what ways do you express your anger?

	Yes	Sometimes	No
Say nothing, but quietly fume	❏	❏	❏
Hit the roof, scream and shout	❏	❏	❏
Attack other people verbally	❏	❏	❏
Attack other people physically	❏	❏	❏
Make a joke out of it	❏	❏	❏
Comfort eat or drink	❏	❏	❏
Stomp around	❏	❏	❏
Hit out	❏	❏	❏
Burst into tears	❏	❏	❏
Be sarcastic and demeaning	❏	❏	❏
Rationally tell the other person	❏	❏	❏
Ignore the other person	❏	❏	❏
Throw things around	❏	❏	❏
Swear	❏	❏	❏
Name-call (e.g. 'You stupid idiot!')	❏	❏	❏
Walk away	❏	❏	❏
Hold your anger in	❏	❏	❏
Block it out and go to sleep	❏	❏	❏

Having completed this list for yourself, make a note of how you've observed your partner dealing with anger, or even better ask them to complete the list themselves and have a discussion about it. Recognize what are the good ways you deal with difference and what are the things you do that might be unhelpful and potentially damaging to the relationship.

Before you even have an argument, notice how difference is dealt with generally in your relationship:

- Do you address misunderstandings and puzzles straight away?
- Does one or both of you not stand up for what you want because you don't want to rock the boat?
- Do either of you keep things in until you're bursting and then explode?
- Are you able to keep things light or do they immediately become highly charged?

Once you've experienced a row with your partner, you can reflect on how you managed it:

- Did you go off into a full-scale slanging match where both of you gave as good as you got, or did one of you dominate?
- To what degree did you shout and swear?
- How safe did you feel while you were arguing?
- Did either of you become abusive?
- Were other incidents from the past that previously had never been discussed suddenly dragged up?
- How much did either of you stay with the facts and behaviour at issue?
- How much did either of you attack each other's personality and judge each other?

All these questions will help you get a clearer picture of how you both deal with conflict. It's up to you to decide if the way you deal with it is appropriate for you. Our only word of caution here is to urge you to make sure that the arguments you have do not threaten the personal safety of either of you: that is, that they are not physically violent and avoid verbal abuse in the form of name-calling, swearing and intimidation.

If you find that you are having very abusive and violent arguments then this is a definite sign that either the relationship needs help, in which case some of the resources at the back of this book may be of assistance, or it is not one you want to continue. Everyone has the right to be treated with respect, and being in an intimate relationship does not mean giving up on those rights.

Respect and difference

The guidelines below will help you in addressing differences that you may have with your partner. You may be holding out for what you really want, but try not to make the other person wrong in the process. Respect them for who they are in the same way that you would expect them to respect you.

- **Describe as opposed to judge**. When we judge we evaluate the other person, and our evaluations are usually based on assumptions about them. Being descriptive is much less emotive.

  For example: 'You interrupted me three times when I was trying to speak' (descriptive) rather than 'You're too pushy' (evaluative).

- **Focus on behaviour rather than personality**. Tell your partner what it is they do or say that is not OK for you rather than what you don't like about them.

  For example: 'When I have a different opinion from you, I've noticed you tell me that I'm wrong' (behaviour) rather than 'You're self-righteous and arrogant' (personality).

- **Be specific rather then general**. Identify why you are unhappy about something and use specific examples. Being specific can support the other person to understand what is happening, rather than leaving them to guess at the problem.

  For example: 'Today, when we were talking about my career, you started telling me what to do before I'd even finished explaining what the issue was' rather than 'You never listen to me.'

When it's time to say goodbye

In testing out your essential requirements one of the conclusions you may come to is that this is not the relationship for you. If your partner is keen to continue with it, that means you have to deliver some bad news.

People tell us they often get very anxious about how to break up with someone. They find it difficult to express what they want to say so the other person isn't unnecessarily hurt. But look at it another way: if you say 'I don't want to hurt the other person', you are putting the other person's feelings before your own and therefore undervaluing yourself and saying they are more important than you. Besides, would you want someone to stay with you just because they don't want to hurt you?

Be sensitive to how the other person feels, but remember: you are not responsible for their reaction. No matter how gently you let them down, they may still be upset or angry; nothing you can do will change that. And be timely. Nothing is worse than letting a relationship continue when you know that you don't want to be in it any more. Let your partner know as soon as possible; that way you can both come to terms with splitting up, begin to separate and move on.

Where does sex fit with testing out?

This is a tricky one. In theory, it doesn't, not in the early stages at least, but in practice it can be hard to say no. The danger is that if you enter into a sexual relationship before you have spent some time in the testing phase, you may be entering a mini-marriage, with, as we noted earlier, all the emotional costs that go with it if you end up having a mini-divorce.

However, what is good in theory can sometimes be hard to stick to in practice, and this whole book is about taking responsibility for yourself: so just be aware of the potential consequences if you do leap into bed before you have had a chance to test out whether you and your partner are really suited to one another.

Sex, love and intimacy

We often confuse sex with intimacy, thinking that if we are having sex with someone, then we are being intimate with them. In fact, physical intimacy is only one level of intimacy. Being fully intimate is also about being prepared to own up to your vulnerabilities, to stop pretending that you are strong or perfect or good. Intimacy is about sharing your real and vulnerable self with another.

We can also confuse sex with love. Some of us have lots of sex in order to reinforce our sense of ourselves as lovable and attractive. Others have sex as a way of expressing love to another. We think that, by having sex, we'll give and/or receive love, which in turn will create intimacy. This is a strategy we adopt in order to get our needs for love and intimacy met. It might work in the short term; but in the long term, because we haven't really opened up to our partner and exposed our true selves, we may feel inhibited and anxious about letting the hidden side of us show. This then impacts on the quality of sex we share with out partner and on how we give and receive love in the relationship.

A better strategy for a long-term fulfilling relationship is to develop intimacy firstly by opening yourselves up to each other, sharing your vulnerabilities and your real selves; from this you will create love.

Ask yourself:

- When you have shared part of your true self with someone, how do you feel?
- When they have spoken honestly and openly about themselves to you, how do you feel?
- Do you feel a connection?
- Do you feel you can trust them more?
- Is there an increase in your sense of fondness and familiarity you have with them?

Honesty, familiarity, an increased connection and trust are all facets of a loving relationship. When you have this, then sex is a great way to share your love and intimacy. And when you are free of all inhibitions, have broken and thrown away all the chains of your past, know, trust and love your partner, just think how your sex life will benefit.

Sexually speaking

Sleeping together and exploring each other sexually can be an important way of checking compatibility before becoming committed to one another for the long term. A good sex life can reflect many strengths in a relationship – effective communication, the ability to let go and be yourself and the ability to recognize and meet each other's needs.

In the last chapter, we asked you to decide what your own guidelines might be for entering into a sexual relationship with a new partner. Our suggestion is that you spend at least one to three months getting to know each other and finding out whether your requirements and needs are being met before entering the pre-commitment phase and becoming sexually intimate with one another. In the end, however, only you can decide what is right for you.

When you get to this point, it is a wonderful opportunity to find out what each of you wants from a sexual relationship and to practise asking for your needs to be met.

EXERCISE: TALKING ABOUT SEX

Here are some things for you to think about and discuss with one another:

- What does romance mean to you?
- What does it mean to your partner?
- Do you want to be watched getting undressed or do you want to undress each other?
- What is your attitude, and that of your partner, to eroticism, pornography, sexual aids?
- How adventurous and alternative does each of you wish to be?

- What are your fantasies? How do you feel about sharing them with each other?
- What does 'making love' mean to you as opposed to 'having sex'? Which do you prefer or do both have their place?
- What fun activities can you share with your partner that allow you the chance to really find out about each other?
- What things can your partner do that make you feel special, e.g. surprises, tender loving gestures, massages?

All of these questions will help you to open up communication around what you like and what you need, which is vital information for the future of the relationship.

It is important that you are able to talk about these things together. Get in touch with the sexual and sensual person within you. Recognize what it is that you pretend when you are making love and whether this is truly who you are as a lover. Let go of the limiting beliefs you might hold about yourself, so that you can open yourself up to full self-expression as a lover and to the joy, openness, connection, fun and love you deserve to have.

Anything goes between two consenting adults, provided it is what you both want. It should go without saying that you need never say 'yes' to things you would rather say 'no' to, just to keep your partner happy, because ultimately, it will be you who loses out.

Sharing your vision with each other

While we believe that living in the present is the best way to enjoy every moment of your life, most people do have hopes and dreams about their future, even if they might never have articulated them. If you are thinking about building a life with someone it is important to find out what their hopes and dreams are and how well these match with your own desires and aspirations.

Building your own vision for your future is very empowering, and then to build one with your potential partner is a great way of seeing how well your lives could grow together side by side.

EXERCISE: YOUR LIFE AND YOUR RELATIONSHIP

In chapter 5 we looked at creating a vision as a means of manifesting what you want for yourself when you were still single and looking to attract a partner into your life. This exercise is a bit different as it's an exercise for you and your partner to do individually before coming together and sharing what you have done.

• Do, be, have: If you had all the money you ever wanted but knew you had only five years left to live, what 100 things would you do, be or have? Most people find that only about 20–30 things pop into their head at first. It's what happens next that can be interesting. Allow yourself to do this exercise over the course of a week and try and reach 100. Then watch out for any surprises.

• Looking back: Imagine it's five or maybe ten years from now, maybe it's 40 or 50 years from now, even; whatever works for you. Write a letter to someone dear to you, in which you are reviewing your life and telling them just how wonderful it has been. What are these things you treasure? With whom did you share them? What have you achieved? What are you grateful for?

Once you both have completed the two parts to this exercise, agree a time that you and you partner can come together to share the things you've discovered. Acknowledge the things that are similar and those that are different, and find out why these are important to each of you.

Then, together, create a vision for how you want your life to be in five or ten years from now, or even further into the future if that is what you want. Create it in a way that feels good for both of you. Write your vision down and sign up to it as a commitment to the life you are creating together. Then set an annual date to revisit it and see what adjustments you want to make to it.

You might also want to represent your vision visually, by painting a picture or creating a collage together. Developing a joint vision is all about sharing your hopes and dreams and inspiring yourselves to take yourself forward into your own exquisite future.

You now have the knowledge that will enhance your ability to find a truly loving and successful relationship. This doesn't mean that you can guarantee never again to get hurt in the process, because old patterns die hard. But by bringing more conscious awareness into your relationships you are making yourself the chooser, and therefore you are less likely to sell out on yourself in order to have a relationship at all costs. If you do become the chooser, then you create a greater opportunity for eventually finding your soulmate.

Being true to myself means I cannot be false to anyone.

Chuck Spezzano, author of *If it Hurts, it Isn't Love*

8

Loving for the Long Haul

Seldom or never does a marriage develop into an individual relationship smoothly without crisis. There is no birth of consciousness without pain.

Carl Jung, psychoanalyst (1875–1961)

You may well feel relief after reading the above quote. At least you know it's normal for love's young dream to get a hard dose of reality after the initial gloss has worn off. It's asking a lot to expect two people, each with maybe 20, 30, 40 or more years of their own personal history and life experience, to walk off into the sunset together with never a cross word between them. And rarely does it happen.

When people say that they have never had a row in their life, we always take it with a pinch of salt, because our experience is that one of them will usually be sacrificing their own needs for the sake of the other – perhaps to keep the peace, or perhaps because that person has forgotten that they ever had needs in the first place. So closely enmeshed are they with their partner that a dependency has grown up that does not allow each of them to recognize themselves as individuals within the relationship.

But that's not you – not now that you've reached this stage in the book. You will have challenges, disagreements, crises; and you will feel stretched at times, maybe even be to the point of questioning why you are in the relationship. This is a common dynamic of any healthy relationship. Long-term love is about creating and relishing the good times and finding ways of dealing with any challenges. The key is to be committed to take on both the good and the not so good times.

By the end of this chapter we hope you will have:

- learned about the power struggles that most relationships get into and how to meet each other's needs without compromising your integrity;
- a clearer understanding of what commitment means for you and how to create it in your relationship;
- identified activities that support the setting up and maintenance of clear and healthy communication;
- learned some tips on how to keep the sexual spark alive;
- created ways in which you and your partner can explore the viability of a long-term partnership.

The sooner you accept that the very nature of your relationship will change once the initial flame of passion subsides, the greater will be your chances of success. It's a well-worn cliché that you have to work at a relationship; and yet, so many of us rarely do so with any degree of awareness. We are shocked when we face our first conflict, and may even feel let down when we find that the person we were so sure was our soulmate proves not to be perfect after all. But then, you're not perfect either, nor is any of us. What we can strive for is to be good enough; and, as part of being good enough, to recognize not only our own emotional needs, but those of our partner, so that we can go some way towards helping them to get their needs met too.

We don't just mean at a simplistic level. 'If I cook, will you unload the dishwasher?' is fine and might be an equitable split of the housework, but 'If you come home for dinner more often, then I'll be willing to have sex with you more than once a week' indicates a whole range of unmet needs, on both sides, which are just not being articulated. No amount of compromise will sort this one out, because the source of the problem, which may relate to all kinds of unresolved business from a couple's past, is not being addressed. And unless they deal with that deeper level, the participants in this relationship may increasingly polarize themselves in their own self-justification and, therefore, blame of the other. We will go on to talk more about effective communication later in this chapter.

Commitment

In the early days of a relationship, working at it is not an issue. Our fantasy is that life will be easy together because we are so much in love. It is when the rose-tinted spectacles start to slip and we begin to see each other in our true colours that the challenge begins.

At that point, unless we are truly committed to the relationship, it is only too easy to walk away disillusioned, feeling hurt and let down. However, if we never truly commit, we will never know the long-term rewards that working at a relationship can bring.

So what does commitment actually mean once you are in an ongoing relationship? Surely, just by the very act of being in it, you are committed? But is that really true? How many of you will have fallen into a long-term relationship, marriage even, without ever truly committing yourself? We talked in the last chapter about the mini-marriage. It's not uncommon these days for couples to move in with each other relatively quickly – 'If it feels good, do it.' That's fine. Who's talking about commitment at this stage? You can always get out as quickly as you got in.

Or can you? Unless you've shut down your emotions or are in denial of them, it's not always easy to leave a relationship without a degree of emotional heartache. A friend of ours commented recently that, in nearly 30 years (from the age of 20), she had had three long-term relationships with a period of two to three years after each when she felt she had needed the time to grieve for the loss and get herself to a point of being ready to start afresh. So, in 30 years, eight years had been spent in relationship recovery of one sort or another.

Would she wish that on anyone else? No. Does she regret any of her relationships? No. But with the benefit of hindsight and with the wisdom she has gained over the years, she might have done things differently. Looking back, and ignoring the first relationship, which was one of youth, she knows that she was not wholly committed in her second relationship and has had to admit to herself that, in her third and longest relationship, her partner was never truly committed to her. Moreover, she probably knew this right from the start.

The more enmeshed the relationship, the harder it becomes to leave it. Some couples have babies – either planned or unplanned – without having discussed properly what they want for the relationship and whether or not that includes starting a family. And so more years go by in an uncommitted sort of way: because even a marriage with children can lack commitment if they are the only reason for keeping it together or tying the knot in the first place.

Many of the couples who used to come and see Ariana were experiencing problems for this very reason: neither partner had ever truly made a conscious commitment to the relationship, and they were not surprised to find that very little now bound them together. If you asked them to say what it was about the other that had attracted them in the first place, many of them couldn't answer the question. They had drifted into the relationship and now they were on the point of drifting out.

Here are some questions you might like to think about if you are at a point in your relationship where you may be thinking about the question of commitment. What can work well is to ask your partner to join you in a discussion using these questions to provoke the thoughts and intentions you both have around commitment.

- What does commitment mean for each of you?
- How would you want to demonstrate your commitment for one another?
- What, if any, fears do you have about commitment?
- How would you know you have your partner's commitment?
- What would you like to be committed to?
- Do each of you share a similar vision for how you want your life to be?
- How do your values differ?
- Do you share similar interests?
- What are the dangers of not committing?
- In saying 'yes' to commitment, what might you be saying 'no' to?

Marriage and the committed relationship

Getting married is signing up to a spiritual, social, legal and some-times religious agreement to be in a relationship, and vowing to maintain certain behaviours and attitudes with regard to your partner and your relationship. Marriage is seen by many people as the 'ultimate' commitment, giving your word to someone in a way that is unique in our society. Yet even possession of a marriage cer-tificate still does not guarantee the level of commitment and love each party will give to the other.

So why get married then? What does being married provide that being in a long-term committed relationship does not? Many people get married because they really love each other and want to be with their partner; but others may be looking for approval from their families or peer group, wanting recognition or status, wanting to fit in and be included, wanting to do the 'right' thing, and so on. Love is often only one reason why people marry, and before you take that step it's important that you are aware of your reasons and the alternatives you have.

With marriage there is a celebration and acknowledgement to the world that you are a couple. In addition, you both have certain legal rights and a social standing. On an emotional level, many people say that being married provides for security in their relationship and togetherness on a different level from cohabitation.

The boundaries of marriage are clearer, tighter and more obvious than in a cohabiting relationship. Marriage is a legal, often religious, contract, and its termination can carry financial, social, religious and emotional penalties. So, when you enter into marriage you take on an increased responsibility to make the relationship work. How many of us who have been married have really thought about that? How many more have actually seen marriage as the goal and once tied the knot actually behaved less responsibly because we think now that we've got what we wanted we can stop trying?

When we invest positive time and energy in something we are usually rewarded, and that increases our motivation and desire to stay involved. For example, if I weed the garden and the flowers bloom more colourfully, as a result I'll feel more inclined to keep weeding the garden. In that sense, marriage is the same as a cohabiting relationship: we reap what we sow and if we work at the relationship we will get rewards from it.

On the other hand, the increased responsibility and legal contract of being married might also mean we stay longer in a relationship that is not good for us, simply because the cost of ending the marriage is greater than the perceived price of staying in it.

We would suggest that you avoid making marriage your ultimate goal, but view it more as a milestone in your relationship that marks the start of a journey together within a different framework from that of cohabitation or simply being in a long-term committed relationship. The framework you and your partner choose is for you both to decide. What is key to ensuring you succeed together is your commitment, which stems from taking personal responsibility for yourself and your part in the relationship.

The power struggle

As romantic love gives way to a different kind of relationship and the chemistry begins to change, we may think our partners have changed too. What has usually happened is that we have begun to see each other in our true colours, and may need to deal with disappointment when we see our partner fall off the pedestal of perfection on which we have placed them.

At this stage we may fall into control and then blame, as we try to turn our partner into something they are not. This can result in anger, frustration or despair and risks killing off the love and satisfaction that existed in the relationship. If we do not find ways to address the issues that are causing the friction, then we may choose to bail out, or simply resign ourselves to how things are and tolerate living in discontent and disillusion.

It's important to remember that this is your relationship and you are responsible for what happens within it, even though there may be times where none of the responsibility actually seems to lie with you. If that is the case, then take a moment to stand back and, from a different perspective, ask yourself:

- What am I doing, or not doing, that is contributing to this situation?
- What could I do differently that might alter things for the better?

Allow yourself to respond to both these questions as honestly as possible. You may find some help in formulating your answers as you continue to read this chapter.

Escape versus active participation

A happy, successful long-term relationship requires each of you to take personal responsibility for actively committing to the relationship. This means staying the course, even when times get rough, and not finding the nearest escape route as a means of avoiding facing the truth about your relationship.

Commitment is about being in a relationship with all your escape routes shut, so you can put your full energy and attention to making the relationship work. Escape routes include such things as unfinished business with ex-partners, career ambitions, bad moods – even what can often seem like innocuous forms of entertainment, if continued regularly, can become a form of passive withdrawal from a relationship as they are the opposite of active participation.

In her book *There Must be More Than This: Finding More Life, Love, and Meaning by Overcoming Your Soft Addictions*, Julia Wright talks about seemingly harmless habits that, in the end, sap our energy, mute our consciousness, rob us of our time and keep us from creating more meaning in our lives and relationships.

EXERCISE: ESCAPE ROUTES

Notice some of the emergency exits that you or your partner might use to disengage from your relationship. Use the list on the opposite page to spark off some ideas. You will no doubt think of others.

- ❏ Overworking.
- ❏ Watching TV all evening – channel-hopping.
- ❏ Having all meals in front of the television.
- ❏ Making children an excuse to disengage from intimacy.
- ❏ Spending all evening talking to friends on the phone.
- ❏ Surfing the internet.
- ❏ Drinking heavily.
- ❏ Over-eating.
- ❏ Keeping busy.
- ❏ Being too concerned with other people's lives.
- ❏ Creating drama.
- ❏ Pornography.
- ❏ Going to bed at different times.
- ❏ Separate holidays.
- ❏ Spending the weekend playing a sport without your partner.
- ❏ Using the family pet as the receptacle for all your feelings.
- ❏ Shopping.
- ❏ Developing emotionally intimate relationships with others that detract from your primary relationship.
- ❏ Sex outside your primary relationship.
- ❏ Filling all your time together with social activities with others.

- What escape routes do you need to close the door on?
- What excuses, activities, situations or people do you use as a means to avoid giving full attention to your relationship?
- How does this impact on your relationship?
- What commitment are you prepared to make to closing down these escape routes?

On the following page are some more questions for you to answer to gauge your level of active participation in your relationship. When you have answered them, think about what conclusions you draw from your answers. What do you want to do differently as a result?

	Yes	No
Do you and your partner acknowledge each other's way of seeing the world without making the other wrong, even if it might not be your way? How do you demonstrate this?		
Do you acknowledge each other's experiences of life without trivializing them? How do you demonstrate this?		
Do you acknowledge each other's feelings? How do you demonstrate this?		
Do you feel heard (not just listened to) by your partner? Do they feel heard by you? How do you demonstrate this?		
Are you and your partner able to communicate your needs and desires to one another? How do you demonstrate this?		
Do you both feel you are equals in the relationship? How do you demonstrate this?		
Do you like each other? How do you demonstrate this?		
Can each of you gauge the temperature of your relationship by being sensitive to its ups and downs and staying alert to any signals that might tell you that something is not right? How do you demonstrate this?		
Would you both be prepared to admit there was a problem in your relationship and not feel too proud to seek help where necessary?		

If you answered 'No' to any of the questions, this could be an area where your relationship could be at risk. Here is a chance for you both to look at your relationship afresh and develop it, rather than hitting a crisis because you have chosen to ignore the problems. Instead of retreating through your own escape routes, how about using that energy to create some strategies for making your relationship work better?

Conscious loving

If you invest heavily now in consciously creating a loving relationship, you will reap the benefit in years to come. One of the ways you can do this is in your expression of love for one another. Each of us has our own different ways of giving and receiving love, and many of us fall into the trap of mind-reading their partner, so don't make any assumptions here. Tell your partner what you would like and don't forget to ask the same from them.

How do you know when you feel loved by your partner? Do they need to touch you or speak to you in a certain way, or do you need them to give you some other form of demonstration of their love for you? What makes your partner feel loved? Are you sure you know?

The 'Five Languages of Love'

In his book *The Five Languages of Love*, Gary Chapman identifies five ways or 'languages' in which we can communicate our love:

- *Words of affirmation.* Verbal compliments, or words of appreciation, are powerful communicators of love. They are best expressed in simple, straightforward statements of affirmation.
- *Quality time.* Looking at each other and talking, giving your undivided attention. That 20 or more minutes of time will never be had again: we are giving our lives to each other. It is a powerful communicator of love.
- *Receiving gifts.* A gift is something you can hold in your hand and say, 'Look, he was thinking of me' or 'She remembered me'. The gift is a symbol of thought and the thought remains not only in the mind, but is expressed in actually securing the gift and giving it as an expression of love.
- *Acts of Service.* Doing things you know your spouse would like you to do. You seek to please your partner by serving them, to express your love for them by doing things for him or her. These acts require thought, planning, time, effort and energy.

- *Physical Touch.* For some individuals, physical touch is their primary love language. Without it, they feel unloved. With it, their emotional tank is filled, and they feel secure in the love of their spouse. The touch of love may take many forms. Don't make the mistake that the touch that brings pleasure to you will also bring pleasure to your partner.

When we choose active expressions of love in the primary love language of our spouse, we create an emotional climate where we can deal with our conflicts and failures.

What if the love language of your spouse is something that doesn't come naturally to you? When an action doesn't come naturally, it is a greater expression of love.

Communication

Being able to talk to each other and speak our own truth openly and honestly is probably the greatest strength any couple can possess. It is the key to unlocking all other challenges that relationship might face. Communicating clearly opens up the potential to maintain and improve our sex lives, deal with conflict and difference effectively, and find ways to keep the relationship rich, exciting and alive.

And yet, probably one of the key reasons why many couples come for coaching or counselling is that communication between them has ground to a halt. Rather than talking to each other, they talk over each other; it's no wonder they no longer feel heard. In fact, the hour spent in the counselling session is often the only hour in the week that they are devoting to each other. For the rest of the time, the escape routes mentioned earlier enable them to avoid facing any of the problems in their relationship, or outside it for that matter. Other annoyances and frustrations are buried deep but with anger simmering just below the surface, arguments can blow up for no valid or apparent reason.

Often, when we have not found a way of communicating what is actually going on for us, it's easier to come home and 'kick the dog' or shout at the children than to acknowledge that life does not seem to be working properly and that we have a responsibility for that.

Agree a regular quality check

Service organizations are always asking for feedback from their customers about their experiences, so why not apply similar principles to your relationship? That way, any irritants can be nipped in the bud – and you both have the opportunity to show regular appreciation of each other.

You can do this as often as once a week, but we would suggest you find an interval that works for you. We know of one couple who have a special breakfast every Sunday where they take the chance to see how each of them think they are doing as a couple. Another couple does something similar once a month; then each year on their wedding anniversary they do a review of what was good about their relationship over the past year and share their hopes and expectations for the coming year.

The next exercise offers a structure that you might find useful to work through as a way of running a quality check over your relationship. Although it might seem rather artificial at first, the more you practise it, the more you will get into the flow of it, and you will realize that it need be no different from a normal conversation.

EXERCISE: QUALITY CHECK

Allow time for each of you to share with the other the following:

- *Appreciations.* What has your partner done in the last week or month that you really admire or appreciate about them?
- *Puzzles and confusions.* What might your partner have done or said that has puzzled you and that you'd like them to clarify? For example: 'I noticed you were looking at the career pages in the Sunday papers and I was wondering if you were wanting to change jobs?'
- *Complaints with recommendations.* This is a chance to voice anything that might be bugging you; however, it's really important that any complaint (negative) is accompanied by a suggestion of

how you would like things to be different (constructive).

For example: 'I didn't like it when you came in late the other night and woke me up. I felt very tired the next day. I'd really like it if in future you would let me sleep.'

- *Hopes and dreams.* Finish your quality check by sharing hopes and dreams that you both have about the immediate and the long-term future.

  For example: 'I'm really excited about the coming week because we have a great weekend planned with the family. Also, I love the fact that we are making such headway with doing the house up, we really are creating a beautiful home for ourselves.'

Make sure you really do listen to one another when you do the above exercise. You might even want to write down what each other has said as a means of validating and recording your discussion. If your partner has a complaint and is seeking a way of resolving it, find out what their real concern is and maintain an adult or neutral approach by acknowledging to them that you hear what they are saying. Whatever it is, it's obviously important to your partner and it is your job to respect that and not minimize its significance – even though it might seem trivial to you.

EXERCISE: THREE TOOLS FOR EFFECTIVE COMMUNICATION

This exercise offers three useful tools you can use in responding to your partner constructively. Even if you can only manage one of these approaches, it is better than nothing. However, using all three will make your partner feel really heard. Then switch sides, so that you have a chance to respond to your partner's concerns.

- *Summarizing*: Paraphrase your partner's message: 'If I've got this right, what I'm hearing you say is...', 'What you seem to be saying is...'. Follow this, first, by checking out: 'Is that right?' and, second, by asking: 'Is there anything else?'. Then finish by summarizing what you have heard.

- *Validating*: 'I understand you might be feeling this way because I know I have been coming home late rather a lot recently.' 'You make sense because I know I do get rather lazy sometimes.'

- *Empathizing*: 'I imagine it's hard to cope when you're feeling so tired.' 'You are sounding rather fed up.' 'It sounds like you're feeling a bit unloved at the moment.' Again follow this up, first, by checking out: 'Did I get it right? Is that what you're feeling?' and, second, by asking: 'Is there anything else?' It's really important to get all your partner's concerns out so that you can address the whole situation and have more chance of reaching a resolution.

Stay clear of the 'blame and attack' game

When dealing with differences, put your own judgments, criticisms, reactions and responses to one side. Why is this important? Blaming, criticizing and judging get us right back into the arena of trying to prove that we are right and in so doing making the other person wrong. Consequently, it leads to defensiveness on both sides and to disconnection – because when we're angry, we simply don't listen.

If you blame me, I have no interest in anything else other than to defend myself by attacking you. When we blame and attack we are seeing the world exclusively from our standpoint and therefore we disconnect from our partner and move away from finding a win–win solution (one that benefits both parties). By contrast, when we maintain a neutral approach in our communication, we are treating both our partner and ourselves with respect and this creates an atmosphere for solving our differences more collaboratively.

Setting boundaries

Boundaries are those invisible walls of protection with which we surround ourselves and over which others may not step without our permission. They are crucial to a relationship's long-term success and lasting intimacy, both for each of you as an individual and for you as a couple if you have children. Boundaries are important to our emotional well-being: they help us to feel safe and secure and help other people to understand where they stand with us.

Children, for example, need to learn that there are times when they cannot have your attention, times when Mum and Dad need to be alone; and if that means locking the bedroom door, then so be it. It is also useful to establish boundaries for their behaviour towards you. Consistently maintained boundaries gives children a structure and makes them feel more secure.

We may also want to set boundaries for ourselves, defining times and places where we are not disturbed either by children or by our partner. Having an hour or so to ourselves several times a week allows us to do our own thing, to reclaim that part of us that is not merged with the needs of everyone around us. This is not about withdrawing or escaping from the relationship; this is about self-care, about taking time out to nurture yourself – ultimately, for the benefit of those around you too. Being selfish is important if we are to thrive and be good role models for others.

- What boundaries do you already have in place and how did you establish them?
- Where do people seem to walk all over you? For example: being treated in a way you don't like; being expected to do something which goes against your beliefs; allowing people to make fun of you. Where do you need to strengthen your boundaries?
- What boundaries would you like to set both around yourself and around the relationship?
- To whom will you communicate your boundaries and how?
- When will you make a start?
- What will tell you that the boundaries you have created for yourself are either working or not working?

Tolerations in your relationship

We talked about 'tolerations' in chapter 4. Here, we want to focus specifically on tolerations within a relationship, most of which develop either because they have been low on our list of priorities or because we have not believed we could do anything about them.

Lots of tolerations become entrenched because they appear trivial and unimportant, and therefore we may feel foolish or petty about challenging them. For example, when he keeps dropping the towels on the floor while she seems to take forever in the bathroom. Yet these small irritations add up to increasing resentment and dissatisfaction that can lead to loss of love and relationship breakdown.

Not dealing with our tolerations causes anxiety and a whole range of physical symptoms, such as tiredness, nausea and headaches. The longer we tolerate something, the more we become resigned to it. Ever heard the story about the boiled frog? If you put a frog in a pan of boiling water, it will jump out; the water's too hot. But put the frog in a pan of cool water and gradually increase the temperature one degree at a time and the frog will adapt, not noticing the gradual increase in heat, until eventually it cannot sustain itself and dies. Rather a depressing analogy, but spot-on in illustrating the impact that tolerating has on our well-being. Do you want to feel alive or to feel dead? If the former, then sort out your tolerations.

EXERCISE: IDENTIFYING TOLERATIONS IN YOUR RELATIONSHIP

Take some time to think about this exercise.

- Make a list of all the things that are draining your energy in the relationship.
- List all the things that you think might be draining your partner's energy in the relationship.
- Are you prepared to commit to doing whatever it takes to deal with these tolerations?

The trouble with tolerations is that we tend to put up with them for far too long – that's why they are called tolerations. So, as soon as you notice something is bugging you, try informing your partner sooner rather than later. So often, what could have been talked about quite calmly and politely at first because it was only a minor irritant can grow into a whole mountain of frustration later on; and then, when we try to talk about it, we can find it almost impossible to stop our emotions from overwhelming our communication. When this happens it is incredibly hard not to blame or judge the other person and you may find yourself in a row over something that, if dealt with earlier, could have remained quite trivial.

In the end, whether we like it or not, we can choose what to change. There is always choice. If it seems otherwise, we may just not like the options that are available to us, or we may be getting something (whether we want to admit it or not) out of keeping ourselves stuck.

- Are you absolutely sure you can't change anything? What alternatives might be available to you?
- What's your fear about not taking appropriate action?
- What do you get out of your current action (or inaction)?
- What impact does it have?
- In agreeing to one course of action, what are you missing out on?
- If you choose not to take action, how can you help yourself to accept your situation and think of ways in which you can reframe it in a more positive light?

EXERCISE: DEALING WITH TOLERATIONS IN YOUR RELATIONSHIP

Here's one way of dealing with something you would like to stop tolerating in your relationship. First, ask yourself what specific behaviour is causing your discomfort and whether it is reasonable to expect that behaviour to stop. If it is, then:

STEP 1: OBSERVE: Tell your partner what it is about their behaviour you have observed. Keep your observation short, clear and descriptive of the behaviour that is annoying you. Do not judge or criticize your partner – simply point out what they have done. Keep the tone of your voice neutral, that is, don't be sarcastic or condescending.

If you do this and your partner does nothing, move on to step 2.

STEP 2: OBSERVE AND REQUEST: Repeat your observation, only this time make a request about what you would like done differently. Don't expect them to know automatically.

Again, make sure you keep your voice neutral, and don't get into blame or criticism. If your partner says 'Yes', then that's great. However, suppose that after a few weeks, the same problem crops up again...

STEP 3: OBSERVE, INSIST AND POINT OUT THE CONSEQUENCES: 'Insistence' and 'consequences' sound like heavy terms, but if something serious is at issue, such as constant heavy drinking or being sworn at, then you need to be able to insist and have some realistic consequences thought out.

If this still does not work, then move to...

STEP 4: LEAVE OR LET GO: 'Leave' can refer to leaving the room or leaving the relationship itself if the issue is more than you think you can tolerate.

Here's an example of this process in action: 'I don't like it when you yell at me when we are having a conversation. Will you please stop doing that? If you are not willing or able to lower your voice, I will leave the room.' The next time this situation occurs, you tell him or her, 'Remember, I don't like it when you yell at me. If you don't stop, I am going to leave the room.' If the yelling continues, you follow through and leave the room.

However, if the issue is something more inconsequential, such as who empties the rubbish bin, you might decide to let go of it. At least you have run it round the block with them and expressed your discontentment in an open and honest way. And, in doing that, notice what is different about the way you feel about your partner and about the thing you were tolerating. You'd be surprised how simply expressing yourself can make a difference to our attitude and feelings about a situation.

Sex and intimacy in a long-term relationship

Why is it that when we are not in a relationship, we seem to spend a lot of time thinking about sex and missing it, and when we are in one, we tend to take it for granted? We're not saying this is universally true, but the more single men and women we talk to (ourselves included), the more we come across this phenomenon. It's not just about sex, of course. What it's really about is that whole package we call intimacy.

What happens when you are in the early phases of a relationship that has become intimate? If you are in a long-term relationship now, how did you treat each other when you first met? Of course, there's usually a lot of physical contact, but what about the rest of it? You will also have had a huge amount of emotional contact that will have come out of being together in a way that you may, by now, almost have forgotten about.

As time goes on, it is so easy to begin to take each other for granted; to stop sharing ourselves, our hopes and dreams, our doubts and uncertainties; to stop expressing our care for each other in the way we once did, so that our partner, although they might know they are loved, may not actually feel loved. This is one of the ways in which intimacy can go out of a relationship through the back door and, as a result, sex becomes just simply OK; satisfactory, but not great.

EXERCISE: HOW IS YOUR SEX LIFE?

If you are in a long-term relationship, how would you rate your sex life on a scale of 0 to 10, with 0 being non-existent, 5 being satisfactory and 10 being mind-blowing?

How would you like it if your score went up a notch or two? Wouldn't that be good?

Of course, there could be a multitude of reasons why sex might not be working for you so well any more, and it may be that you need to consider seeking the services of a psychosexual therapist. But for most couples going for relationship counselling who require help in sorting out their sexual apathy, the problem is often their lack of real intimacy: those caring behaviours and expressions of love that were so readily offered in the early days without expecting anything in return.

Can you remember what these were? Well, here are some of the things that couples often do together during those early heady days when they love and feel loved and want to connect emotionally to one another:

- think of ways in which you can please your partner;
- be interested in your partner, wanting to know their view on things;
- speak to each other on the phone daily when not together;
- plan new and exciting things to do together
- enjoy simple pleasures together like walking or cycling;
- cook special meals;
- cuddle on the sofa;
- hold hands;
- do the washing up together;
- massage with oils;
- french kiss;
- take a bath together;
- book a surprise evening out or weekend away;
- walk for miles together, hand in hand or arm in arm;
- feed each other delicious food;
- write each other poems or love notes;
- text messages of affection;
- turn up with small and thoughtful gifts;
- send flowers;
- compile a CD or tape of meaningful songs that remind you of special times together;
- look into each other's eyes for hours on end;
- sit quietly or with calm music, appreciating each other's presence;
- leave a flower or love note on your lover's pillow;
- send a gemstone the colour of your partner's eyes to them through the post.

EXERCISE: EXPRESSIONS OF LOVE

Think back to when your relationship first began and write your answers to the following questions in your journal.

- How did your partner demonstrate their love for you?
- What are some of the ways in which they demonstrate their love for you now?
- What are some other things that you would like them to do for you now that would make you feel loved and special?

Once you and your partner have each listed your answers under these headings, rate the importance of each action from 1 to 5, then swap them and discuss those you will find easy to do, those more difficult and those impossible to do.

You don't need to do the impossible, so if there are any you can't negotiate a way round, remove them. Then start working your way through the list in any order, trying to do at least one or two a day for your partner for the next month. Notice any resistance you are feeling, but just carry on doing them. At the end of the month, get together and talk about the experience of doing this. See if you can agree to do it for another month.

Harville Hendrix, in his excellent book *Getting the Love You Want*, calls this 're-romanticizing'. Steven Covey's book *The Seven Habits of Highly Successful People* talks about creating an emotional bank account: each loving act is like a deposit in the account, and it is important to keep the account in credit. Whatever you want to call it, it is a common technique that relationship experts use with couples and is a wonderful way of learning to reconnect emotionally with one another.

Make sure you acknowledge your partner when they do offer one of these expressions of love. You will be amazed at the positive changes that start to happen as you begin to focus on what you can do (as opposed to what your partner should be doing) to improve the intimacy within your relationship.

Keep dating...

No matter how long you have been together, and particularly when children come on the scene, keeping the fun and excitement alive is a really important part of maintaining intimacy. It's very easy to let family demands come first, yet the satisfaction in your relationship is fundamental to your well-being, both as individuals and as a couple.

Having a weekly date that is quite separate from friends, family and children is a chance for you to share an experience that is just between the two of you. Go for a meal together, go for a walk or use one of the other examples that you came up with in the above exercise. Call them dates, or whatever you want to call them, and commit to them.

... and keep talking

Above all, keep talking. The more you communicate and express your feelings to one another, the more you take your partner's feelings into account and the more you share openly with each other the greater the chances of success within your relationship. One of the happiest couples we know has been married for over 30 years. Want to share the ingredients of their success? Here's what they said:

- a bath together every evening, often with a diary, to discuss the day's events and plan what's coming up;
- mutual respect;
- daily laughter;
- gentle teasing, but being aware of the other's feelings and knowing when to back off;
- eating meals together without the television on;
- having interests they share and ones they don't;
- lots of talking and sharing;
- having agreed separate time on their own, free of family and relationship commitments.

Admittedly, their children are grown up now and they are both retired; but they have had their share of ups and downs. These simple ingredients have provided the glue that has kept them bonded throughout what has turned out to be a loving and enduring relationship. Who could argue with that?

References and Resources

On relationships

Barbara de Angelis, *Are You the One For Me?* (Thorsons, 1992)

Rhonda Britten, *Fearless Loving* (Hodder & Stoughton, 2003)

Gary Chapman, *The Five Languages of Love* (Northfield Publishing, 1992)

Gay Henricks and Kathlyn Hendricks, *The Journey to Co-commitment* (Bantam Books, 1990)

Harville Hendrix, *Getting the Love You Want: A Guide for Couples* (Owl Books, 2001)

Harville Hendrix, *Keeping the Love You Find: A Guide for Singles* (Atra Books, 1993

Charlotte Kasl, *If the Buddha Dated* (Penguin/Arkana, 1999)

Seana McGee and Maurice Taylor, *The New Couple: Why the Old Rules Don't Work and What Does* (HarperCollins, 2001)

Martin E.P. Seligman, *Authentic Happiness* (Nicholas Brearly Publishing, 2003)

Chuck Spezzano, *If It Hurts, It Isn't Love* (Hodder & Stoughton, 1998)

On developing effective communication and relationship skills

Harriet J. Lerner, *The Dance of Anger* (HarperCollins, 1999)

Harriet J. Lerner, *The Dance of Intimacy* (Perennial, 1997)

Joseph O'Connor and John Seymour, *Introducing NLP: Psychological Skills for Understanding and Influencing People* (Thorsons, 1995)

Marshall B. Rosenberg, *Nonviolent Communication: A Language of Compassion,* (Puddledancer Press, 1999)

Ian Stewart and Vann Joines, *T.A. Today: A New Introduction to Transactional Analysis* (Lifespace Publishing, 1993)

On flirting and sexuality

Tracy Cox, *Supersex* (Dorling Kindersley, 2002)

Peta Heskell, *Flirtcoach* (Thorsons, 2001)

Barbara Keesling, *The Good Girls' Guide to Bad Girls' Sex* (Bantam, 2002)

Lou Paget, *How to Be a Great Lover* (Piatkus, 1999)

On personal development and growth

Jean Illsley Clarke and Connie Dawson, *Growing Up Again* (Hazelden, 1989)

Steven Covey, *The Seven Habits of Highly Effective People* (Simon & Schuster, 1989)

Foundation for Inner Peace, The, *A Course in Miracles* (Viking, 1996)

Lynn Grabhorn, *Excuse Me, Your Life is Waiting* (Hampton Roads Publishing, 2000)

Sue Annis Hammond, *The Thin Book of Appreciative Inquiry* (CSS Publishing, 1996)

Susan Jeffers, *Embracing Uncertainty* (Hodder & Stoughton, 2002)

Byron Katie, *Loving What Is* (Random House, 2002)

M. Scott Peck, *The Road Less Travelled* (Random House, 1990)

Anthony Robbins, *Awaken the Giant Within* (Pocket Books, 1993)

Sanaya Roman and Duane Packer, *Creating Money: Keys to Abundance* (H.J. Kramer Inc., 1988)

Martin Seligman, *Authentic Happiness* (Freepress, 2002)

Neale Donald Walsch, *Conversations with God* (Hodder & Stoughton, 1997)

Nick Williams, *The Work We Were Born to Do* (Element Books, 2000)

Marianne Williamson, *A Return to Love* (Thorsons, 1996)

Marion Woodman, *Addiction to Perfection* (Inner City Books, 1982)

Judith Wright, *There Must Be More Than This: Finding More Life Love and Meaning by Overcoming Your Soft Addictions* (Broadway Books, 2003)

Websites

Relationships

www.therelationshipcafe.com
Ariana and Mary's website, offering workshops, telephone classes, relationship coaching and support. We would love to hear from you; contact us via email at: info@therelationshipcafe.com.

www.coupleconnect.com
Debra Munn and CoupleConnect cards.

www.relate.org
The website of Relate, for information about relationship counselling.

www.relationshipcoachinginstitute.com
The international relationship coaching training organization.

www.marygregory.com
Mary's site for personal and organizational effectiveness through the development of successful relationships.

Personal support and growth

www.bacp.co.uk
The British Association of Counselling and Psychotherapy.

www.coachu.com
The Coach University website; includes a directory of coaches.

www.coachfederation.org
The governing body for coaches; includes a list of accredited coaches.

Personal development training courses

www.outlooktraining.org
Delivers a series of courses that focuses on developing personal confidence, accessing and utilizing your inner potential, and overcoming fear so that you can create what you want in your life.

www.hoffmaninstitute.org
Offers an eight-day programme designed to release negative conditioning from the past and enable you to access your personal power.

www.landmarkeducation.com
Delivers a programme known as the Landmark Forum, designed to bring about positive and permanent shifts in your personal relationships, confidence and productivity

Dating

www.realconnection.com
Ariana's unique personal introduction service for professional men who are seeking a partner for life.

www.match.com
An international site with useful screening and personality testing for participants.

www.guardiansoulmates.com
A UK site with thorough preference and compatibility screening.

www.datingdirect.com
The largest UK dating website.

Flirting and sexuality

www.flirtcoach.com
The site of Peta Heskell, expert flirt, author, coach and speaker.

www.diamondlighttantra.com
The site of Leora Lightwoman, a teacher in tantra who offers a selection of courses and workshops and also tantra coaching.

www.tickledonline.com
The site of Tickled sells a variety of sex aids and toys and offers a helpful service.

Acknowledgements

We'd like to thank our partners, ex-husbands, lovers and dates for the fun, love, laughter and tears we have shared, and whose presence in our lives have given us such rich insights and life experience as a basis for us to learn, grow and contribute to others.

Thank you to our coaching clients, whose journeys we feel privileged to have shared a part of.

Thank you to our friends and family, particularly our parents and Sarah Nee, for your never-ending support in our lives and in the writing of this book.

We are particularly grateful to Sally Bibb for her constant encouragement and positivity about our endeavours, and to Andrew Pegg, whose commitment, time and energy in reviewing our work was relentless, and whose inspiring feedback really added a perspective and rigour to our text.

Thanks also to Kevin Boyd, Peter Davis, Mike Tomlin, Mary Clarke, Pauline Esson, Carol Golcher and Michael Olsen for their support and unstinting belief in what we were trying to achieve.

We'd also like to thank our own coaches and teachers who have inspired us over the years and supported us to assimilate the knowledge, awareness, confidence and insights that underpin our work. Namely, Talane Miedaner, Aboodi Shaby, Tony Wiseman, Suhith Shivaneth, Judy Hargreaves, Josie Gregory, Paul Barber, Paul Tosey, Sue Knight, Ian Ross, Ian McDermott, Arielle Essex, David Steele, Ishbel Daniel, Marianne Craig, Alma Neville, Kate Edmonds and Merry Graham.

And, finally, we would like to thank each other – writing this book has been an amazing journey for us both, we've learned loads, had a ball and discovered an enduring friendship in the process.